Andy Russell's Adventures with Wild Animals

Andy Russell's Adventures with Wild Animals

with Illustrations by Harry Savage

Hurtig Publishers
Edmonton

Hurtig Publishers Ltd.
10560-105 Street
Edmonton, Alberta

ISBN 0-88830-199-5

Printed and bound in Canada
by T. H. Best Printing Company Limited

Contents

Introduction

The watcher of animals whose interest goes beyond casual observation to a desire to uncover their secret lives finds that his interest never peaks, but continually increases. For the longer he looks, the more he is aware of how much is left to learn, and of how our lives are tied to the lives of animals in nature's intricate patterns. Though we are inclined to view mankind as vastly superior in every way, sometimes not even recognizing it as an animal species, we are inseparably a part of all living things on the face of this planet Earth. The greatest difference between ourselves and other animal life is our intelligence. We *know* that we know, and other animals just know.

But we have no monopoly on thought. Although intelligence varies between species and between individuals of any one species, animals can and do adjust remarkably well to problems and unusual circumstances never before met along their trails. To explain it away as instinct is either deliberate misconception or pure laziness. Their undoubted ability to accommodate changing conditions and meet emergencies often spells their survival.

When one has spent a long time in wilderness country mingling with wildlife and watching wild animals work out the patterns of their lives, one becomes increasingly aware of parallels. They too know happiness and sorrow, the serenity of peace and the trauma of fear. They too suffer from stress, often reacting to it irrationally just as we do. Anyone who has watched a mother grizzly or coyote guard her young in the face of threatening danger, or caress them while indolently loafing under a warm sun, knows that they too love their offspring. When one watches otters play in utter abandon for the sheer love of it, one is very sure that they are supremely happy in their wild environment and are expressing joy, as we do at such times.

When one watches grizzlies to the point of literally living with them over many months in the wild country of their choice, it becomes very evident that here are animals with just as much individual character as human beings. There are the timid and the bold, the cranky and uncompromising, those that are mild and some that are a great deal smarter than others. All are very quick to sense an advantage.

When Yellowstone Park was originally formed to protect the game from market hunters, the much harried grizzlies became aware of its boundaries within a year or so, took shelter there, and were much more comfortable and unconcerned when they met now disarmed humans.

The grizzly bear is probably the most maligned and misunderstood animal on the face of the earth. Ever since the white man set foot on its range, the grizzly bear has been feared, harried and hunted. Great portions of the big bear's habitat have been destroyed forever. Even within national parks they are sometimes driven over the brink of stress resistance and react with uncharacteristic, irrational violence. Yet undoubtedly there have been thousands of times they could have killed, but chose to let us go in peace.

Faced with man's completely unreasonable desire to eliminate it from the face of the earth, the coyote stands as a monument to razor-sharp intelligence. In spite of unremitting exercise of rifles, traps, snares, dogs, motor toboggans, all-terrain vehicles, airplanes and the most lethal poisons, the coyote still survives in good numbers, expanding its range and even reclaiming it in some of the least likely places.

In the place called the Valley of Ten Thousand Smokes by the old California Indians, the vast metropolis of Los Angeles now stands with its conglomeration of high-speed roads, buildings and millions upon millions of people under a sometimes choking pall of smog. This was once coyote country. For a long time they were kept out, but now there are coyotes living amongst roaring traffic; raising their young amidst human habitation; eating mice, rats, fruit, garbage and whatever else can be found. Sometimes they howl and people are frightened for the safety of their children, raising an awful hubbub with city authorities.

One can imagine the coyotes secretly grinning at the irony of it. For, through survival of the fittest in the face of hate, unremitting warfare and blind illogic, man has defeated his own purpose by creating a super-breed of coyotes far more intelligent and sometimes vastly more destructive than those he could be dealing with had he chosen to control rather than eliminate. In this instance and in others we have got our just come-uppances!

In the great theatre of the wilds there are colour and drama, scintillating drama so packed with action and the aura of mystic ritual that it reaches the stars and sometimes makes a man sob with emotion at the beauty and wonder of it. What better illustration than the mountains echoing and ringing with the bugling of rutting bull elk under a full moon? If man, through his dalliance with destructive forces and his greed, eliminates this, he will have lost touch with

9

his past, his present and perhaps even his means of survival as a species.

There are those who say endangered creatures can be saved in zoos and game farms. How can we know the awful trauma and boredom of a wild animal confined in a cage? We can't, unless we have lived in such confinement ourselves. It would be far more humane to let species die out and erect bronze tablets *in memoriam* to remind us of our short-sightedness.

All the stories in this book illustrate the needs of animals in relation to the needs of man. I suppose it all boils down to their right to live; the morality of being able to hold their rightful places in the vast tapestry of nature's life chains; the great necessity for these to remain unbroken for the good of all. It is as simple as the need for a peaceful place to sleep, something fit to eat and the privilege of singing to the moon when the spirit moves us. It is as complicated as human competition can make it.

Paramount in all of this is the obvious need for greater understanding and sympathy on the part of man.

Once wild animals lived without us. Now they must live with us. For our own good, may we prove the superior wisdom we claim is ours by finding a way to make this possible.

Andy Russell's Adventures with Wild Animals

Sage

It was late April and up on the head of the South Fork it was snowing — not unusual in the Rockies in springtime, but this was no ordinary storm. It had started at daylight with big flakes whirling on a northwest wind, and by noon the new fall was fourteen inches deep, wet and heavy. It continued unabated, whirling and driving in blinding eddies in the lee of a great rock wall over a mile long and 2,500 feet high along the east face of the Continental Divide, the crest of the great North American watershed.

The day before, an atmospheric disturbance had occurred off the Pacific coast eight-hundred-odd miles to the southwest, when a low pressure area drifted inland from the ocean across the Oregon coast, dumping heavy rain. Around this low pressure centre, the air currents swung in a clockwise whirl, sucking up warm air from farther south, which passed over the cold sea water, gathering more moisture before curling inland over Washington and British Columbia. Because it was warm, it rose higher and higher, then spread its wings and flew inland. As it travelled, gaining velocity, it cooled and

13

dropped till it hit the cold, snow-draped phalanx of the Rocky Mountains. There the moisture it carried came down as snow, the major part of it settling on the highest ground along a fifty-mile front.

At daylight, forty-eight hours later, the storm was over and the sky was clearing. The sun came up to light a snowy wilderness, only the sheer face of the cliffs showing dark in an otherwise unbroken ocean of white. New snow lay forty inches deep in the sheltered places, over several feet of old snow. The timber was draped with it in sculptures that took on myriad shapes.

The big basin below the great cliff is flanked on the north and south by buttressing ridges sloping down off the summit of the Divide. It is carpeted by big timber along the lower edge of the talus fans formed by loose rock eroding from the cliff face. To the east it opens into a valley, where the south fork of the Castle River flows north towards its confluence with the west and north forks.

There was absolute quiet at first, but as the sun climbed and warmed, there came the soft swishing of snow slipping from bowed branches of the trees. The cliff face gradually darkened as melt-water ran down the naked rock from above. Water ran into a crack behind a projecting knob fifteen hundred vertical feet up, and began to melt the ice collected there. This ice was helping to hold the knob to the cliff face in a fissure it had made as it froze. Now as the ice melted, the weight of the projecting rock became too much to bear, and it suddenly cracked loose with a sound like a rifle shot. The released boulder came down in a sheer drop for a hundred feet. Its several tons hit a projecting ledge with a boom like thunder, exploding it in many fragments that fell on the next long leap towards the slope below. The roar of the descent triggered an avalanche high on the south face of the flanking ridge to the north.

Snow came pouring down a ravine, filling it to

14

overflowing, and slamming into big trees growing along its flanks. With a thunderous roar that boomed and echoed through the mountains for miles, millions of tons of wet snow moving at incredible velocity wiped out great trees, hundreds of years in the growing, in an instant. The vibrations triggered other avalanches until the cannonade of sound filled everything and the mountains seemed bent on reducing themselves to rubble. But the quiet returned, and the white mountain flanks showed several long brownish scars, where the slides had gouged down to old snow and earth in their wild plunges to lower ground.

The lives of small animals — pine squirrels, martens, snowshoe hares and porcupines — were snuffed out in the wink of an eye. A trader rat, sleeping in a big hollow stump in the path of the initial slide, woke up to find himself tumbling like a chip in a rolling barrel. The stump bounded into a tree, shattering, as the snow came to a stop, and the rat was miraculously spared, though somewhat befuddled by finding itself suddenly out in the open in blinding sunlight. It had been dormant all winter, but had been active between naps for several days. Now it was wide awake and it crept fearfully under a slab of broken wood to ponder this sudden change of scenery.

Under ten feet of hard snow and six feet of earth on the flank of the ravine, a mother grizzly awakened and stood up, her two cubs crowding under her belly as the mountain shook under the weight of the avalanche. When it subsided, she was restless; as though making up her mind, she went to the entrance of the tunnel leading into her nesting chamber and began to dig. The cubs, frightened by the noise of the slide and unable to see in the velvet blackness of the cave, found themselves in a storm of flying snow shovelled back by her big feet. With mounting excitement, they squirmed and snuffled, alternately being pushed back and crowding up against her haunches as she dug. Suddenly they were blinded by a brilliant shaft of sunlight as she broke through the crust. All three emerged, blinking and sniffing, into the open. What had looked like a lifeless wilderness now held the warm-blooded presence of grizzlies, their heavy fur coats glistening in the sun, and their noses working on the gentle air currents blowing up the slope into their faces. At best grizzlies' eyes are short-sighted, but their wonderful noses told them everything instantly. There were smells of snow, wet earth, freshly broken wood and bruised spruce, fir and pine needles.

Silver, the mother, was predominantly black with a glistening mantle of silver guard hairs running from her face back along her shoulders and flanks. Her claws were white as ivory; five dully gleaming, curved scimitars fully five-and-a-half inches in length on each forepaw, grown long through no use during the winter months. Sage, her male cub, was a miniature, fifty-pound replica of his mother, and his sister, Balsam, the same size, was a rich golden blonde with dark chocolate-coloured ears, feet and half-moon shaped spot on top of her shoulder hump.

For a while the big mother bear stood motionless, feeling the warmth of the sun and letting her eyes adjust to the brilliant light. A little cat's paw of wind shimmered the fur over her shoulders and this seemed to animate her, for she ambled downslope with the rolling stride so typical of grizzlies. The cubs trailed single file behind her, sometimes breaking their stride with a short bound or two to keep up, for bears never trot. They are two-gaited animals — a walk, or a gallop that can sped up to an astonishing thirty-five miles an hour.

Her way took her down past the wreckage of the stump, where the trader rat was crouched under the big splinter, and the breeze brought the pungent smell of him to her nose. She paused a moment, then walked up and turned over his cover. The rat had heard her coming and when she exposed him, he

shot away toward a tree and up it. The grizzlies watched him go with no attempt to catch him.

They wandered on down the hard-packed snow of the avalanche track. The she-grizzly had no destination in mind; she was simply following her nose. Ordinarily, she would have stayed in her den for another three weeks. She was not particularly hungry, for she still carried fat from the previous fall, and her digestive tract had shrunk from months of disuse. The cubs were fat from her rich milk, and they still suckled every two or three hours. They crowded up to her in request now as she paused to sniff at some fir boughs lying in a tangled heap. She squatted there, and they reared against her broad chest, kneading with their front paws as they fastened onto her dugs and sucked. Their combined weight overbalanced her, and she sagged over on her back, while they continued sharing her milk.

That afternoon was spent exploring the slide. At sunset, she led the cubs back up to the den, which she sniffed but did not re-enter. Fifty yards farther up the ravine, she found a mat of bear grass exposed where the avalanche had gouged deep on the edge of a drop-off. There, she and the cubs spent the night, the mother on her belly with her big nose cradled on her paws, and the cubs cuddled up close to her flanks, snoring contentedly in her warmth.

Next morning, when the sun came up to turn the snowy peaks rose against the blue of a cloudless sky, the mother grizzly was breaking trail down the crest of the ridge toward the valley. In places the wind had whipped the new snow away, exposing the hard-crusted old snow of winter storms and here the travelling was easy. But, as they went down past timberline, she was ploughing along flank deep. She went steadily, her powerful shoulders and haunches rolling in cadence with her stride. Behind her, the cubs trailed along, bits of snow clinging to the fur of their faces, bellies and legs. As the slope pitched down more steeply, she sometimes

18

plunged ahead, and the cubs were hard pressed to keep up as they made scrambling leaps from one gouge of her track to the next. After one stretch of this faster travel, when neither one of them could see their mother half the time, Sage and Balsam began to whimper in complaint.

Silver stopped on the edge of a little clearing and waited for them. They crowded up to nurse and rest, while the distant thunder of more avalanches rumbled through the mountains, and the forest around them was full of the sound of water dripping. Then they resumed their journey.

Evening found them in a thick willow patch close by the creek in the valley bottom. Silver ploughed her way down to it for a big drink, before they slept among the willows in a nest hollowed out of the snow.

At dawn the bears were on the move again under paling stars, but now Silver took to the easier going of the creek bed, splashing along down its stoney channel. The water was icy and the cubs did not like it. They kept as much as possible to the shallows, occasionally diving into the deep snow for a short distance. Paying them little attention Silver kept on for an hour, until her feet, tender after the long winter in the den, began to hurt on the sharp rocks. She climbed the bank on the edge of a big clump of heavy spruce to let the cubs suckle.

There, a vagrant puff of breeze brought a tiny bit of scent to her nose. Instantly she was alert, searching for another whiff, but the little eddy of wind did not come back. Getting to her feet, she went into the timber, slowly circling among the big boles of the trees with her head up and her nose working. Then she caught the smell again and knew where it came from.

With seeming casualness, she went over to a mound of snow held up by a big deadfall, and began to dig. As she dug, the cubs crowded up alongside her, bouncing with excitement. Her paws suddenly broke into a chamber

19

hollowed out under the log, and there, in the middle of a nest of grass and boughs, stood a small black bear, humped up, spitting and hissing in alarm. With no more effort than a house cat would employ in taking a chipmunk, and just as quick, she grabbed him by the loose skin on one cheek and dragged him out. His bawling wail was abruptly cut off as she shifted her grip to his neck. Holding him down with her front paws, she quickly killed him, while the cubs leapt about in a frenzy. Paying them no heed, she tore open the carcass and fed, then buried what was left in the snow and lay down beside it. When she and the cubs left three days later nothing remained but a few fragments of bone and tufts of hair scattered here and there.

A week later they were out of the mountains. Silver lay in an aspen grove atop a bluff overlooking a valley. The snow had not been as heavy here and there were only old greyish drifts remaining in the hollows and lee sides of the hills. New grass was showing pale green on the slopes facing the sun. Silver had spent several hours trying to fill up her hungry belly on this skimpy fare, and now she lay with the cubs, her nose working on a smell of carrion wafting up on the wind from the direction of a ranch headquarters below. Occasional sounds — cattle bawling, the barking of a dog — came to their ears. The smell of carrion was tantalizing, for there is nothing a bear loves more in spring than well-ripened meat. Besides, she was ravenous; the long ramble down the Divide through the snow had afforded little to eat apart from the black bear, and the cubs' constant demands added to her gauntness. But her hunger did not blunt her caution, for she was acquainted with men and knew something of the dangers that went with them.

Six years before, a freshly weaned two-year-old alone for the first time in her life, she had wandered into this valley and found the carcass of a cow. Such a find is a treasure to a grizzly, and for several days she fed on it undisturbed. But

20

one morning just after sun-up, a man rode in over the rim of the hollow in which it lay, taking her by surprise. When she reared to look, his horse spooked and shyed and this probably saved her life, for by the time the rider got his mount back in control, she was running for the timber. He drew his rifle as he stepped down, and sent a bullet cracking viciously past her ears, speeding her up. Another spattered earth up under her belly. A third slammed into a rock as she shot behind it. Just as she came to the edge of the trees, a fourth bullet struck her on one haunch, spinning her hind end around hard into a tree. She went down roaring and biting at herself and rolled behind a log. Then she gathered her feet under her and plunged out of sight.

Behind her, the man followed cautiously for a ways along a blood trail that soon thinned out and lost itself among the dead leaves and forest debris.

The wound was shallow and not serious, for it missed the bone and large blood vessels, but the leg was stiff and painful. It gradually came back to full strength, but the imprint of the experience never left her. Now Silver lay with the cubs flattened out beside her, sniffing the wind and waiting.

When it was almost dark, she got up and led the way downhill, keeping in cover along a draw. She went slowly, pausing often to test the wind and listen. When she came to flatter ground, she circled wide of the buildings and corrals, keeping among some scattered stringers of willows and aspens. Sage and Balsam were excited and nervous, but they made no unnecessary moves, trailing at their mother's heels and mimicking almost every move she made.

The sky was overcast, threatening rain, and the damp air made conditions perfect for her marvelous nose. She caught the sweet smell of bedded cattle chewing their cud and swung around them on a route that brought her to the top of a bank by a little creek. It was now velvety dark, a condition

21

that bothered her not at all as she led the way down to the water and then up along the stream. A quarter-mile from the buildings she came on the refuse dump, where the rancher had left several newborn calves, dead from exposure during the storm.

She ate most of one where she found it, ripping it apart and devouring bones, hide and all in big hungry gulps, while the cubs tore and tugged at another. Somewhere down wind, a coyote, picking up their scent, yapped and howled. This triggered a flurry of barking from the ranch dog at the buildings, and a few moments later lights flared, and a truck motor added its noise to the night.

Silver did not linger. Picking up the carcass of a calf crosswise in her mouth she headed up the slope behind the buildings. At sun-up, she and the cubs were well hidden in the heart of a willow thicket, sleeping off their heavy feed.

For a week she never strayed more than a mile from the buildings. The bare ground hid the tracks of her nightly forays, and although the ranch dog knew about the bears, his master, preoccupied with attending to his calving cows, never realized that three grizzlies were his guests. When the dead calves were finished, Silver left, heading back into the mountains.

The warm weather was cutting away the last of the snow on the lower slopes; the receding drifts were closely followed by grass and the green leaves and golden blooms of glacier lilies, favourite food of grizzlies. Now that vegetation was plentiful, Silver and her cubs followed their noses aimlessly, carefree as the mountain winds, fed bountifully by the great wilderness that was their home.

They shared the forest glades and mountain meadows with mule deer, moose, elk and other bears. On the higher open slopes, bighorns were feeding on the new growth, their winter coats in rags as they shed the old hair. Proud rams lifted their heads to watch the grizzly family as it passed.

Early June rains set off a great surge of new growth; now the grass was waving in the wind, pea-vine was climbing in the brush and wildflowers were a colourful riot of bloom everywhere. From the ranches in the east, herds of cattle were driven into the mountains for the summer and soon scattered in all directions in every valley.

Among the yearlings from one ranch there was a steer suffering from bovine diptheria; the first in a series of steps culminating in a cruel drama dictated by Man seeing his profits go astray.

What possible difference could that one steer make, amongst those hundreds of cattle? It made a difference, because viruses get passed along, and soon there were other sick cattle. In time they began to fall dead here and there. Not many of the fifteen hundred head of cattle died, and, in the heavily timbered, folded country, those that did were not readily apparent to the lone man who rode for the stock association that owned them.

When he found the first carcass, there was little left of it, for Silver and her cubs had located it first. He marked down "One yearling killed by a grizzly," in his little book, for he was a meticulous man, fond of keeping facts. Then he found another — a carcass that had been fed on by black bears. They leave different signs, and again the stubby pencil came out and there was another note of a bear kill.

The word came to the ranchers and they summoned Old Bill, a wiry, grizzled mountain man, who had hunted and trapped mountain country for more years than he bothered to count. After some bargaining, he agreed to kill bears for a wage plus bounty — ten dollars for a black bear and twenty for a grizzly.

His face gave away little about his thoughts as he packed grub, camping gear and two fifty-pound steel traps on his horses, but he had an abiding contempt for his employers; indeed, for anything to do with what he called "farmers".

On a bend of Lynx Creek, he made a snug camp under some big trees on the edge of a meadow, and proceeded to have an unhurried "look-see", as he called it.

He was one of the last of his kind — a child of the wilderness — an eagle-eyed wanderer and practiced observer who missed very little. His term *look-see* fitted perfectly, for he saw more at a casual glance than most men would in a month, and he understood the smallest sign.

At the end of his second day of poking around the valleys and ridges, he was heading back to camp on his little buckskin mare. As she shuffled along at a running walk in the warm sun, he confided to her, "Some bunch of farmers! Bear kills!" and spat a stream of tobacco juice with unerring accuracy all over an unfortunate frog perched on the edge of a pond beside the trail. That surprised creature leapt into the water with a splash, while Old Bill went on, "One big ol' grizzly — likely a he one — a momma grizzly with two cubs and maybe a dozen black bears, all eatin' on cows dead of Gawd-knows-what! More cows sick and more bears likely joinin' in the fun!"

The mare waved an ear at this unusually long speech, whereupon Bill subsided into silence with a disgusted grunt. He would keep his knowledge to himself, for it was nothing to him if he took bounty money for killing bears that were not killing.

So the stage was laid.

Grizzly country is complex, with deep, folded features covered with timber. Merely looking is not enough; one must know where to look and what to look for. Above all one must learn how to move. Man has lost this art granted him by nature; his motions have become jerky and unco-ordinated, telegraphing his presence and his intentions. Watch a bear, a deer or a coyote; unless startled into precipitate flight, its motions are always smooth-flowing.

The person wishing to learn about wild animals must learn to move like them. Only then will he or she begin to understand them.

It probably never occurred to Old Bill that he was something of a naturalist. His success as a hunter and trapper had come from long exposure, for he had known no other way of life since he was a small boy. Taking life was the way he made his living, but in that role of a predator he was a keen student of nature. He had to be, or he would have been forced to find means of support in work he abhorred, like digging post holes or tending cows.

One evening some time later, I sat by a campfire with him and listened while he told of that summer of bear hunting. He was rarely loquacious, but that night he loosened up, considering himself in the company of a friend who shared his environment and respected his choice in living there. It was a story of bloodshed, cruel and without pity; yet it was revealing and marvelous in its account of patience, keen observation and endurance. I sat enthralled, prodding him with a gentle remark or a question when he began to lag. It was past midnight when he finally rose, stretched himself and grunted an end to the story. Then he headed for his bed with that peculiar springy walk developed by having travelled thousands of miles on snowshoes. Though his stride had shortened, he carried himself with a looseness and grace most men half his age could not emulate. He reminded me of an old wolf beginning to show the wear of many winters.

The sickness among the cattle that summer was by no means an epidemic, but enough of them were dying to attract the bears. When the hot weather of July came, carrion was not nearly as attractive to them, for hordes of bluebottle flies turned the carcasses into masses of squirming maggots, which bears do not like.

The dead yearling Silver found by the Carbondale River, was alive with maggots, so she dragged it into a riffle to let the current wash them off. Directly below, the trout filled up till they bulged, while Silver and her cubs fed on the stinking steer remains. She buried what was left in a damp, heavy layer of leaf mould under some big cottonwoods on the bank, where a big male grizzly found it and fed on it.

Old Bill came upon what was left, built a log pen with an open end around it, and there he set one of his big traps. Silver, being aware of the interference of the male, didn't come back. The big male was not old for lack of wisdom, and promptly abandoned the claim, not being hungry enough to want the bait upon smelling man around it.

A black bear came snooping, and put its foot in the trap. Bill promptly killed it, rolled its carcass into the pen and reset the trap. Two days later he had another black bear — another scalp. Two black bears being equal to one grizzly, he was uncomplaining about this turn of events. Bounty was bounty and it made no difference to him what kind of bears provided the scalps for his collection. So far he had found no sign that any of the cattle had been killed by bears. That might have stayed true all summer had there been any kind of berry crop that year.

A late frost had killed most of the blooms on the saskatoon and huckleberry bushes, so the bears did not have their usual mid-summer source of feed. Beef became more attractive than usual, and finally the big bear made a kill.

He was crossing a meadow by Lynx Creek, a mile or so above Bill's camp, one morning at daylight, when his nose and ears picked up the smell and sounds of approaching cattle. Flattening out on his belly behind a little clump of brush, he watched a bunch of yearlings file into the open. The wind was from the cattle to the bear, and they were ambling by unconcernedly twenty yards in front of him when he launched his charge. Three bounds put him among

26

them. A swinging paw caught a heifer in the face with such force that his claws penetrated the frontal bone of her skull, cutting off her wild bawl of panic instantly.

He was feeding on the heifer when he heard a horse blow its nose in the timber behind him, and he quickly sought the cover of the trees. Shortly after, the trapper rode into the clearing to stop and sit his mount looking at the kill. He reined the buckskin around the clearing, reading the sign. He saw the gouge marks of the grizzly's claws where the big animal had launched its charge. A few yards away there was a big track on the dirt of a pocket gopher mound. What had occurred, what bear was involved and every detail of the incident was as clear as newsprint to him. Without dismounting, he rode back to camp, saddled a packhorse and picked up a trap.

That afternoon, he was back at the kill, and with customary dispatch proceeded to construct a V-shaped pen of dead logs around it. Crossing the logs at the apex of the V, he wired them together. The logs at the open end of the enclosure were wired to two upright stakes and a crosspiece was fastened across the top. More poles were piled to form a crude roof, thus making the open end the only way to get at the carcass. Then Bill cut and dragged in a green log about eight inches in diameter and ten feet long to which he chained and wired the trap. It was set with a screw clamp for it was a massive thing weighing close to fifty pounds. He placed it directly in the door of the pen with little sharpened stakes arranged upright around it to ensure that the bear would put its foot directly on the tripping mechanism. Throwing a thin layer of old leaves and grass over the trap, he stood surveying his handiwork and found it good.

When the stars came out that night, the clearing was lit faintly by a quarter moon hanging over the mountains. Faint and far off among the ridges south of the creek, a great horned owl hooted its question to the night. The call was answered by another in some big cottonwoods up the valley. Then the quiet came back. One moment the little meadow was empty, and the next a great bear stood with his nose swinging as he tested a tiny draft of moving air carrying the smell of his kill. Except for the movement of his head, the grizzly stood like a statue for several minutes, then silently moved in closer. His nose told him the man had been there, and the pen was something he had encountered before. He was suspicious but hungry.

Circling the pen, he examined it closely. Going to the back of it, he hooked the claws of a front paw in a chink between the poles, testing it and finding it solid. He pushed his nose close to a crack and sniffed the powerful smell of ripening meat. Circling around to the front, he stood with his head over the trap, smelling iron and man. Directly in front of him, one short step away — tantalizingly close — was his kill, but his cunning held him back, the nudging of caution turning him away.

Again he went to the back of the pen and rearing, put his forepaws on top. With a spring of astonishing agility, he leapt up, and the roof of the pen groaned and shifted a bit under his weight. Another move put him directly over the trap. Suddenly his weight broke the supporting crosspiece and it collapsed under him letting the whole roof fall in a heap. The trap clanged shut on a front paw, but also on the end of a pole, so that when he leapt away the paw slipped out. Snorting angrily, he approached again from the side and hooking his paws on the logs, heaved back with a powerful tug, tearing the supporting stake from the ground. He grabbed the carcass with his teeth, dragged it out into the open and then stood over it with a rumbling growl. Taking it by the neck, he hauled it away into the timber and proceeded to fill up.

When the old trapper came back in the morning and surveyed the wreckage of his labour, he snorted angrily through his nose, not unlike the grizzly, but he was far from quitting and went to fetch his other trap.

This time he wired what was left of the carcass to the foot of a tree and rebuilt the pen over it, using the tree for an anchor. He set one trap as before, but buried its mate in the ground, artfully concealing it. It was a formidable lay-out with nearly a hundred pounds of steel lying cocked and ready.

But the weakness of traps lies in the fact that they are completely non-selective. When the grizzly came back late that night, there was a black bear struggling to break free of the mighty shackles clamped on two of its feet. After hearing and smelling the hopeless fight his lesser cousin was waging, the grizzly faded away into the timber.

So it went with Bill's efforts to trap the only bear that was killing cattle. Almost inevitably black bears, hungry and scrounging for whatever they could find to eat in the absence of berries, walked blindly into his traps. The challenge to capture the killer grew, but the trapper was working against heavy odds, for not only were the black bears numerous, but the grizzly's cunning was growing rapidly.

Meanwhile, Silver and her cubs managed to avoid the trapper — not by intent, but by sheer good luck. Because she had no desire to compete for territory with the old male, she ranged high on the slopes above the valleys.

One day the three came into a hidden basin at timberline. There the summer was held up by altitude and the winter's accumulation of snow, so the vegetation ranged from early spring at the edges of lingering drifts, to summer on the shelves and terraces sloping down to a little lake in the basin's middle. Sometime ages past, a great piece of the mountain had broken off to deposit a huge mass of boulders reaching down to one end of the lake. This was flanked by alpine meadows now covered by masses of mountain flowers, and occupied by a colony of marmots living among the rocks and feeding on the flora. The lush vegetation, fed by the seeps and fountains of many springs, provided ample forage for Silver and the cubs.

The marmots, while interesting, hardly counted in the grizzlies' diet, as whenever the bears appeared, sentinal marmots posted on boulders gave off long-drawn piercing whistles of alarm. One morning, however, Silver, seeking shade rather than marmots, led the cubs into a narrow, grassy ravine by a stream. Coming over a little rise, she almost stepped on a feeding marmot. Letting out a gurgling squeal of terror it fled, but Silver was on it in two jumps, pinning it under a big front paw. She killed it with one crunch of her powerful jaws and devoured it, while her cubs crowded in close trying to get a share. The fat meat whetted her appetite for more and her nose led her to the marmot's hole, where she began to dig, sniffing and grunting, until she could hear the chirps and squeals of a nest full of kits. But the marmot's nesting chamber was between two big sunken rocks with a boulder for a roof, and although she was close enough to almost touch the kits, there was no way she could get at them. Tired and hot, she backed out in somewhat of a bad temper. She smacked Sage when he came up to her begging to be suckled, and going to the stream, she drank and lay down to soak in the icy water.

The basin was an idyllic place for other game as well as for Silver and her family. They shared it with a small band of mountain goats, a few mule deer bucks and bull elk. Like the bears, these animals sought the deep shade during the heat of the day; the goats in nooks and crannies high on the cliffs where their marvelous eyes commanded everything below, the rest among scattered groves of timberline trees.

One close, hot afternoon, the bull elk were lying in and around a spring bubbling from the ground beneath some big, ancient larches. Two of the bulls were bedded in the soft, wet muck directly below the trees, while the remainder sprawled in various attitudes of repose on the adjoining meadow, where little zephyrs played over them. A sudden storm rolled in from the west, blotting out the sun like a curtain suddenly drawn across it, and accompanied by rolling reverberations of thunder. A few big raindrops heralded a downpour, but the elk did not move as they enjoyed the coolness.

Then came the sharp report of a lightening bolt closely followed by a blast of thunder that shook the ground and brought them to their feet — all but the two under the trees. Their heads sagged; their noses pressed into the mud. They had been instantly killed by lightning that had struck the top of one of the trees, torn a strip of bark in a spiral pattern to the ground and gone out through the roots into the wet ooze of the spring.

Silver found them there next morning, a lavish feast on which she and the cubs fed till they bulged. She dragged both carcasses out onto the meadow and buried them there under a layer of forest debris and sod. Such a bonanza of feed provided by sheer accident held the grizzlies close by as long it lasted. They alternated their feeds of carrion with grazing on the lush grass growing thick and rich on the spring-fed meadows. The cubs were growing fast and Silver's gauntness smoothed out with new fat.

On a warm morning they climbed up a big steep snowdrift sloping down from the foot of the cliffs to the first scrub near timberline. At the top, Silver sat down on her broad rump and slid at a break-neck pace on what seemed a bone-shattering collision course to the rocks and trees at the bottom. The cubs followed her without the slightest hesitation as though such sliding was an everyday event in their lives. They went with the recklessness of drunks, but when disaster seemed inevitable, all three came up on their feet, set their claws and skidded to a stop. Again they climbed for another round. A pair of Clark's crows sounded off at their intrusion and goats stood on miniscule ledges far above, looking down at this carefree play of grizzlies.

Rising heat made the sliding pall, and Silver led the way higher to a big crack, where the drift sagged away from the cliff face. She lay down in a convenient hollow melted out by reflection of the sun. Rolling over on her back with all four paws in the air, she stretched out luxuriantly in the cool snow. The cubs, after poking around curiously examining this place, soon followed her lead.

Occasionally clouds blew in over the ranges, tearing out their bottoms on the jagged peaks and spilling their rain, sometimes gently and sometimes in roaring downpours accompanied by violent lightning and earth-shaking barrages of thunder. Because of the elevation and the deep winter snow, the summer was later here; the huckleberries bloomed late and missed the killing frost. Not long after the elk carcasses had ceased to be anything but a lingering smell, bits of shrivelled hide and scattered bones, the berries began to appear — sweet, luscious fruit providing Silver and her cubs with a wealth of delicious feed.

Silver's fur had been ragged and sunburnt, but now her new coat was growing in — glossy with gleaming guard hairs shining in the sun. The cubs were rolling with fat — smaller models of their mother's mold — each wearing new coats, with fur thickening and lengthening as the days of late summer shortened into early fall.

The grizzlies did not have the berries to themselves, for the deer and elk ate them, as did the coyotes, foxes and birds. Two black bears showed up to enjoy the feast and by mid-September the berry crop was thinning out.

Suddenly the weather changed. Temperatures dropped under a great cloud mass blowing in from the northwest, and it began to snow. The storm lasted less than a full day, but it dropped a sixteen-inch blanket of heavy wet stuff.

When the sky cleared and the sun came out, animals reappeared, hungry and looking for food, but the bears found scanty pickings. The ground squirrel population was at a low ebb in its cycle, so what normally would have been a quick transfer of interest from berries to digging up hibernating squirrels did not occur this year.

Fate is a fickle mistress, and every living thing on earth flirts with her every day of its life. Weather is always an unknown factor that changes the directions of lives more than does any other natural condition; the circumstances control the success of birth, the abundance of feed; and daily changes spell comfort or discomfort. Even the rugged grizzly has been known to freeze to death in its winter den through lack of sufficient insulating snow cover. What assists one may destroy another; when the snowfall is deep and crusted, it may kill those depending on graze, but it will mean comfort and security for bears. Sometimes very little will tip the balance for or against any animal. Sometimes fate is lightning swift and sometimes cruelly slow, but it is always there.

So, because she was hungry and could find nothing to satisfy her appetite, Silver struck out for lower ground with her cubs. A mile or so below the basin, she came out on a promontory overlooking the Carbondale River, and stopped to read the wind. It told her of nothing but wet green timber and snow, so, with a soft grunt to the cubs, she moved on down to a well-marked trail leading down-river.

By dark they were miles from the basin, the cubs beginning to lag a bit behind as Silver's long stride ate up the distance. Their guts were growling in emptiness, when their noses picked up the galvanizing smell of meat in an open timbered park. It came from the carcass of a steer buried by the old killer male. Mingled with it was the faint, unmistakable odour of man.

The big male had killed it on the day before the storm, and by sheer luck, Bill had found it while it was still warm. By now Bill's pursuit of the killer had become a fixed determination to wipe out this bear. It was a challenge that meant more than money; it was a contest, a battle of wits in which the old mountain man felt his reputation was at stake.

Bill fetched his traps, but this time he built no pen over the carcass, which was lying in a close quadrangle formed by fallen logs. With cunning and patient attention to detail, he buried his traps, chaining them to trees and camouflaging his work to match the surroundings so artfully that even his practiced eyes had trouble locating it. After brushing the whole location with a piece of the raw hide to cover his smell he went back to his camp.

That night, when the grizzly came back, he stood downwind in the falling snow reading the air with his nose. He might have been blind for all he used his eyes. The absence of a pen meant very little; the buried traps so carefully hidden even less. That superlative nose picked up the smell of steel and man over the smell of beef even though conditions were unfavourable in the wet falling snow. Without taking another step in the direction of his kill, the big bear swivelled on his heels, and faded away like a ghost among the trees. He climbed straight up a flanking ridge out of the valley, and at dawn stalked and killed another beef in a pocket along a small creek two miles away.

Bill woke suddenly in the small hours of that morning when his tent collapsed on him under the weight of snow. Grumbling to himself, he crawled out into the storm and managed to prop up one end of it, making enough room to sleep, and then went back to bed. At daylight, he looked out on a dreary world and set about repairing his camp. He found that his horses had pulled out for lower country, leaving him afoot.

After a hurried breakfast, he set out on their trail through snow that came up to his knees. In spite of their hobbles, the horses had been travelling steadily since daylight and the trapper knew he had a long day ahead of him. Stoically, with a patience born of experience, he trailed them, not hurrying or pausing to rest, knowing that sooner or later he would catch up. It was six miles or so and early afternoon before he came up to the missing animals, and bridled the buckskin. Removing the hobbles, he drove them back to camp, arriving there miserably cold, wet and hungry. By the time he had eaten supper it was getting dark, and, wondering if he had the killer grizzly in his traps, he went to bed listening to the cheery tinkling of his horse bells.

Up among the towering spruce Silver stood within three steps of the dead steer, the nudging of caution making her pause, for she could smell the faint scents of both the male bear and the man, though the snow had almost erased them. The cubs came up on each side of her and Sage took a step past; she anchored him in his tracks with a gruff coughing sound. Torn between caution and hunger, she stood still for a moment. Hunger won. She stepped forward over a log, and instantly the ground exploded under her foot, and the night was suddenly wild with her great bawl. She leapt straight up with a trap fastened to her paw. The chain jerked her up short as she plunged away, snapping her around, and a moment later the second trap slammed shut on a hind foot.

When a wild free thing as big and powerful as a grizzly suddenly finds itself shackled in steel, it is frightful. For as long as life remains, the animal fights, roaring and plunging — an awesome cataclysm of conflict between mighty muscles and ungiving steel. It is an obscenity — a desecration of nature's great gift of life.

Silver ripped the bark from all the big trees within reach, chewed one, five inches in diameter, completely off, and ripped the rotten dead logs to shreds, mixing them in a mulch of torn-up earth. When the cubs came close, she

35

roared at them with a savagery that they had never known, and they retreated into the timber to circle and bawl in fright.

Shortly after daylight, the trapper, still a mile down the trail, heard Silver roaring. He kicked his horse into a trot, and near the grove where the set was located, he tied her to a tree and proceeded on foot, rifle at the ready. He saw the bear in the trap, and knew that he had been beaten again, but he coolly took in every detail of the surroundings. A flash of golden fur showed between two trees beyond the trapped bear. The rifle came up, steadied, and roared, and Balsam went down in a heap, shot through the heart. Then Sage appeared on a galloping run and the gun swung after him. A branch brushed the barrel just as the trigger was let go, and the bullet merely grazed Sage's front foot. He tumbled end over end, coming back onto his feet in a whirling change of direction. This sudden turn saved his life, for the bullet that would have torn his heart out cut through the flesh along his ribs under his right foreleg, and emerged in front of his shoulder. With a high-pitched roar, he bit at the wound and went down in a twisting roll that carried him over the bank. He fell twice his length into two feet of icy water.

Bill sprinted to the top of the bank, but the young grizzly was gone, only a bloody trail showing in the snow on the far side of the river. Methodically he turned and shot the trapped mother bear through the head. He stood looking down at her, and though it had been a profitable morning — two grizzlies and one probable — he was disappointed.

He skinned both grizzlies, for their hides were close to prime, and after hanging the skins in a tree, he mounted his horse to take the track of the wounded one.

What he expected to be a short trail turned into a long one.

"I trailed that little bugger for most of two days," he told me at that evening fire almost two years later. "Losin' him went plum agin the grain, but I finally gave up when the snow melted. He weren't hurt very bad, but I figured he would die durin' the winter. He sure wouldn't be diggin' much with that hurt front leg and two broken toes. My first shot hit him in the foot, and the next just raked him, missin' the bone. He was some lame, but used the foot."

Biting off a fresh chew from a plug of tobacco, he ruminated in silence for a while, then put out a glowing coal on the edge of the fire with a well aimed spurt of juice and continued, "But the little son-of-a-gun was tough — he didn't die. I seen his track several times since. Outside toes of his right front foot is twisted in, crowdin' each other, and he toes in a bit more with that paw. Last time I seen his tracks was up on the summit of the South Fork headin' into the Park. Never seen them since." Then as a sort of rueful afterthought, he added, "And I ain't got that big ol' killer yet! Hell of a note! It seems like he learns faster than me. But I'll hang up his hide some day."

If he did, it was not in this world. Some weeks later the old man rode into a rancher's yard and sat with his head down and his shoulders hunched up, not making any effort to get off his horse. As the rancher's wife opened the door to call him in, he fell in a heap, dead before he hit the ground. A tough old heart had just quit beating.

Two years after Old Bill's death, I was out riding, looking for some horses on our ranch land that borders the northeast rim of the Park, when, in some soft mud, I saw a fresh grizzly track that brought me up short for a closer look. The outside toes of the right front paw were warped inward, the two long claws almost touching at the tips with the third. And the paw mark toed in a bit more than the left one. Could it be the same grizzly Old Bill had wounded and lost? I remembered that long evening, the campfire smoke drifting up through towering spruce to the glittering canopy of stars. I would have bet my best horse it was the same bear.

He'd be six years old now, a big, heavy animal (his tracks showed that), and I wondered if he would be able to stay out of trouble in the ranching country.

As it turned out, this was the beginning of a long and unique association between this bear and our family. We lived for twenty years in the same territory, and we came to know each other well, each completely accepting the other's presence.

Don't misunderstand; in no way was this sharing of territory an intimate thing. It was a very tenuous acquaintance as far as contacts went, but we felt his presence. We were aware of sharing a piece of wild country, relatively unchanged since the buffalo had wandered across it, in a spirit of mutual interest that entertained no conflict. The great animal came and went with utter caution and secrecy. We rarely saw him; only his great paw marks let us know he had passed by.

Like people, some grizzlies attain full maturity later than others and Sage was one of these. He grew into an enormous bear. At full growth his tracks measured nine and one-half inches across the pads of his front paws. When he stood at full height on his hind feet, he was over eight feet tall. Heavy with fat in the fall, he must have weighed close to nine hundred pounds.

One evening I was sitting atop a hill not far from our house, overlooking a wide expanse of the ranch. There were elk and moose in sight and my glasses were roving when I caught a glimpse of what looked like the back of a moose showing through some willows about half a mile away. The animal was moving toward a little meadow, appearing and disappearing. When it stepped out into the clearing I saw that it was Sage.

His coat was burned into a rusty red by the spring sun, and my ten-power binoculars revealed every detail of him as he grazed from one clump of new, lush herbage to another.

All grizzlies feed largely on vegetation, and Sage was no exception. He was particularly fond of the abundant glacier lilies that bloomed in the aspen groves, and he stripped the whole plant; flower, stem, leaves, all but the bulb, from the soft leaf-mould. He was a sort of self-appointed sanitary engineer, seeking and avidly devouring every dead animal, whether it was wild game or domestic stock. Apart from picking up the occasional newborn fawn, elk or moose calf, he never killed any of the larger mammals.

He didn't stay on our ranch all the time, but ranged over a wide expanse of country, from the rugged mountains of northern Waterton Park to the Waterton River east of us. He regularly visited a big ranch between us and the river, crossing a busy highway to get to it, and, though he spent considerable time there, the owners weren't aware of his presence for some years.

One night in late June as I was driving home I reached a place where the road climbs around a ridge overlooking a deep canyon. As my car lights swung around the curve, they suddenly lit up a huge grizzly jumping across the ditch onto the road. I stood on the brake and gave a short blast on the horn. At that he leapt away toward the canyon below, and there came the metallic scream of barbed wire slipping through staples as he hit the four-wire fence. Grizzlies are usually very adept at negotiating fences, but Sage was in a tearing hurry. Next morning I went back to find thirty yards of our boundary fence flattened, the posts broken off and tufts of silvertip hair caught in the barbs. No doubt he had been mighty put out at the indignity, and I paid him a silent apology while thanking my stars that I had not hit him.

When Sage first came to the ranch, our four boys ranged in age from four years to fifteen, and our daughter wasn't a year old yet. To tolerate a grizzly on the same playground as a family of constantly roving children might seem sheer insanity to many people, but from the time they could walk, ours were always aware of bears. We schooled them to respect the big animals but not to fear them. The two things we impressed in their minds were never to run and never to attempt to climb a tree if they came upon a bear of any kind. For running only provokes pursuit, turning the bear's curiosity into anger, and a tree is a dead-end trail. A black can squirrel up one much faster than a man, and though popular belief denies it, a grizzly can also climb if it so desires.

As the years passed, and the youngsters grew up in an environment shared with bears, they rambled, camped, fished, hunted and explored toward ever widening horizons. Occasionally they encountered the big animals, and though the meetings were brief, they generated an atmosphere of adventure that brought the kids home bright-eyed, bubbling with excitement as they spilled the story in words that tumbled and ran into each other. Very rarely did they have close quarter encounters with grizzlies, for they usually went in pairs or groups and there'd be enough noise to warn the bears of their presence.

They must have been close to Sage, no telling how often, but never did he threaten them. On occasion there would be a brief flash of him, a snort and a crashing of brush as he left only his great paw marks to identify himself.

When they were small they had a dog, a collie, that grew from an awkward pup into a big, heavily furred companion with a dignity of monumental proportions and a deeply ingrained sense of responsibility. We called him Kip. His surroundings must have been akin to a dog heaven, with great freedom and privileges most dogs never know, but his life was not easy. Keeping track of four kids kept him busy; they were an independent lot not inclined to run in a flock.

Heavy aspen forest surrounds our home with thick undergrowth, and visitors were often appalled at the idea of letting youngsters loose in such a wilderness. They were safe when Kip was there though, and he was always in the yard when the younger ones were wandering around. He had an invisible line drawn, and when they reached it, he would just walk around them, holding them back with his bulk. Sometimes his efforts sparked stormy protest, but this never ruffled his dignity, or destroyed his cheerful long-nosed grin, and pummelling small fists in his thick fur seemed to amuse him even more.

Kip was never a trouble-hunter when it came to bears; he'd stand them off if they tried to enter the yard, but he'd never pursue them very far. There may have been confrontations between him and Sage, but we only ever knew about one.

The three oldest boys, Dick, Charlie and John, had been fishing in Cottonwood Creek about a mile from home, and were returning on a trail which wound through timber and meadows along the slope of the hill. Because they were tired, they were quiet. Suddenly they were aware of a monster bear standing on the edge of a patch of saskatoon berry brush only a few steps ahead of them.

Upon hearing their footsteps, Sage reared for a look, towering over them. Quickly Kip stepped between the boys and the bear and stood barking. Probably because this procession had aroused his curiosity, the big bear stepped forward onto the trail, and for a few moments the picture was frozen except for the movement of the steadily barking dog.

John, at the back of the line, was the first to move, but he only backed into the screening greenery beside the trail to stand peeking fearfully out at his brothers, the bear and the dog. For a few long moments, it was a stand-off; then the grizzly turned on his heels and was gone.

The rest of their trip home was made in record time, and, upon their arrival, the adventurers recounted the experience while fairly vibrating with excitement. All but Kip. He just stood panting through his long grin, his tongue protruding a bit farther than usual, but his great dignity intact. He might have been saying, "We met a grizzly, but the kids did alright. They got a little excited, but they didn't run."

Anyone looking at him would never have guessed that he would have given his life to protect them without a second thought. There's an old Indian saying that bravery comes from the heart. If so, Kip had a big one.

The years passed, the youngsters grew apace and Kip became old too soon. One day he passed from our life in the rolling hills under the mountains, where streams wound clear and shining through meadows and aspen groves. He was mourned and missed, for he had been part of our family for a long time.

Our next dog, a German short-haired pointer that we got as a four-month-old pup, was something of a contrast. We called him Seppi, and he quickly proved to be a wonderful companion; a natural hunter and a canine extrovert who provided much fun as well as some headaches. Seppi rapidly grew to be a big dog with a great nose, wonderful co-ordination and speed. There were things he had to find out for himself: a porcupine taught him a painful lesson that never needed to be repeated, and a big mule deer doe gave him an unmerciful beating that taught him to leave the deer alone.

Bears, however, were his passion. If one showed up in the vicinity of the buildings Seppi would launch a red-eyed, roaring attack. If the bear chose to turn and fight, he was up against a master of the game, for Seppi would feint and dodge any lunge, and the bear would find himself bitten in the slack of his furry pants. This, mixed with the unholy howling, generally resulted in the bear beating a scrambling retreat up the nearest tree.

Naturally, I was concerned about the day he and Sage would tangle, and for this reason we kept him in the house at night. He accepted this privilege with imperious aplomb and insisted on sleeping in my favourite chair.

One evening, out for a walk with Seppi, we came upon Sage's fresh tracks in a muddy place at the outlet of a small lake. The dog's reaction to grizzly scent was completely different to anything I had observed before. He came to a rigid point, not unlike that he would use on grouse, but far more tense. The short hair over his shoulders stood straight up in a bristly ruff, and a menacing growl rumbled in his throat. He seemed to be instantly aware of an animal far different from an ordinary black bear, and I wondered if he had already met the big grizzly.

On my command to stay, he sat down on the toe of my boot, whining and baying, his whole frame trembling with excitement. It was as though he knew the danger, but wanted to accept the challenge. I stroked him and talked to him for several minutes, calming him down before we moved on toward home.

Seppi and I came to know each other in a dog-man relationship that was most unusual. I trained him, and he schooled me in many things associated with the world of nature. His superlative nose told me much that the sharpest eyes could not see.

Many times after that we encountered Sage's tracks and my dog's reaction was always the same — something far more than just interest; a seeming awareness of a mighty adversary. He would pace ahead of me reading the scent, the hair standing up on his shoulders, and we would trail the bear through fiercely difficult places and conditions. Thus I was able to study movements and habits of the grizzly where the sign would have been almost invisible without the dog.

It was sometimes amazing to discover the things that drew the grizzly's attention. On one occasion we found a place where Sage had spent some time digging for a tiny pocket gopher, following and uncovering its shallow tunnel

44

for yards. It was impossible to tell if he caught it, but it looked as if the grizzly's motivation was a whim of fancy and curiosity rather than hunger, for such a small animal would provide little food.

Sage loved to eat ants, and many times we came upon what was left of a rotten log or stump that he had torn apart in search of its inhabitants, the fragments showing the marks of his great claws.

Once I found a place where he had surprised and killed a beaver among some aspens by a pond. All that was left was a slight smear of blood and a few tufts of fur on a skiff of snow.

Another day, trailing his big paw marks through an early fall of snow, I read the story of how he had taken a snowshoe hare. Going into the wind, he had obviously seen the animal crouched in its hide in a tuft of slough grass along the edge of a swamp. There was no apparent shift of stride or attempt to stalk it — he just walked up to the hare, and plucked the mesmerized animal from its bed with no more effort or fuss than he would use to pick a mouthful of berries.

Trailing him was like reading a book written in a unique kind of script, revealing and totally fascinating. Although we rarely saw him, he taught us much about grizzlies in a way that was matchless.

The years passed and I had long since ceased to worry about Sage and Seppi declaring war on each other, for the dog seemed satisfied with my judgement. But one day in early June of Seppi's eleventh year, all hell broke loose.

Seppi was nearby as I worked in the yard, when suddenly his head came up, and with a fierce growl, he shot into the timber at top speed. My first thought, that he had smelled a black bear, was quickly dispelled when I heard the whistling snort of a grizzly followed by the snarling roar of the dog. The brush crashed, indicating a tearing run that was obviously going over and through, rather than around, any obstructions.

Within a hundred yards or so, the bear turned, and I could hear the two of them mixing in a fight, roaring at each other like nothing else on earth. Racing to the house, I grabbed a rifle and ran in pursuit, yelling to Seppi to come back. They were off again before I could get close enough to be heard, and after a couple of hundred yards they turned on each other once more.

I trailed that running fight for nearly two miles before it faded into the distance. It was a hot day and the sweat was running into my eyes as I struggled to hold my breath and listen. It was no use. My heart was pounding, and I was shaking with exhaustion as I turned back sick with the feeling that my dog was gone forever.

Two hours later I was sitting at my desk writing a letter, when I heard a whine at the door. When I opened it, Seppi staggered in, glassy-eyed with exhaustion, his breath sobbing from tortured lungs. I looked him over and marvelled, for aside from a groove on his shoulder where a claw or a sharp stick had scraped down to the skin, there wasn't a mark on him. He stood for a few minutes, then just collapsed in his tracks. Carrying him to his favourite chair, I rubbed him and talked to him until his breathing gradually slowed down, and he became more relaxed. Then he went to sleep.

He slept for most of two days, waking only for brief periods, and then he seemed to recover; but he was not the same dog. The heart seemed to have gone out of him. Whatever had happened out there among the timbered hills had been too much, for about two months later he suddenly became semi-paralysed. The sun was going down as I carried him outside to the edge of the hill in front of our door. He seemed to rally, then sagged into a fitful sleep. I left him for a while; when I went back to him he was semi-conscious, but did not recognize me. He whined as though in pain, and tried to drag himself down the slope. It was obvious that a great dog had reached the end of his trail. Seeing him suffer was unbearable, so I helped him over the threshold with a merciful bullet — the hardest thing I have ever had to do.

Sage was becoming an old bear. Each fall, during or after a snowfall in late October, we would see his big tracks crossing the ranch as he headed for the mountains and his winter den. Every spring we watched for those familiar marks again, and when we found them, the picture of greening-up time at the foot of the Rockies was somehow more complete.

One spring we will never forget for several very good reasons. It had been a fairly open winter with only short cold spells and less than the normal amount of snow. February and March were very mild, but in late April the weather map got sadly mixed up, and a blinding blizzard whirled in out of the north. Over a period of ten days, it snowed nine feet — a paralyzing storm anywhere, but a real killer in the ranching country.

When the grizzlies emerged from their dens in mid-May, they found themselves looking out over a white wilderness with insufficient feed for snowshoe hares, to say nothing of bears. So they ploughed their way down to lower ground, and we found ourselves hosts to more of the big animals than we had seen sign of for many years.

To add to the abnormality of conditions, one day in June it began to rain; a warm heavy downpour more like a tropical storm than the kind we usually get in the Rockies. On the second day of this deluge the rain was accompanied by a heavy north wind that uprooted great stretches of timber for miles. There were places where hardly a single tree was left standing. In thirty-six hours it rained fifteen inches and the country was swimming in the worst flood in over fifty years.

After the storm stopped in late afternoon of the second

day, I was in the workshop behind the house when I happened to glance through the open door just as a whole procession of grizzlies came out of the timber. A big brown female was in the lead, followed by a pair of well-grown two-year-old cubs, and trailing them was the familiar bulk of Sage. The bears must have been travelling on ground unfamiliar to the lead female, because they were only thirty yards from the kitchen door when they stopped. Sage had arrested them with a sudden snort. Although he was uncomfortable, he was obviously loath to leave because of the sow bear. He suddenly towered up on his hind feet to full height, then swivelled around to lope back the way he had come. The mother bear was of no mind to go back, and boldly led her cubs through the yard within twenty feet of our house. We thought we had seen the last of them.

After dark a heavy ground mist fell, blanketing everything. My wife Kay and I were reading by the fireplace in the front room, when our daughter Anne, who had been busy with some project in the cottage a hundred yards away, came bursting in, her eyes wide with excitement, to say that she had just met the female on the trail between the houses. The bear had been within a few feet of her, but beyond some gusty snorting had made no threat.

A short while later, Anne's little black terrier blew up a storm of barking on the veranda, and when I investigated, I found the sow standing just outside the circle of light thrown by the outside lamp. Somehow the long rays of light cutting into the fog from our front windows had separated her from her cubs. She was calling to them to cross the brightness, but they were afraid to. For a while we were treated to a grandaddy of a domestic argument. To some it would have been terrifying, but we found it so unusual and interesting that it never occurred to us to be afraid. Finally the bears must have sorted out their differences for everything quieted. As I drifted off to sleep I was thinking of

48

Sage and wondering when we would see him again. As it turned out he was not very far away.

Next morning the sun came up warm and bright under a cloudless sky to light up a dripping world of water drops glistening thickly on everything. I stepped out on the veranda with my binoculars, and almost immediately I spotted a most unusual sight. Sage, the sow and her two cubs were flattened out snoozing in the sun in the middle of a little clearing about four hundred and fifty yards along the slope below our house. Picking up my camera, I went for a closer look. Approaching quietly against a feather of breeze, I sneaked to within a few yards of the sleeping grizzlies before I became aware of a fifth grizzly patrolling the edge of the trees near them. This was a young male, perhaps four years old, obviously interested in the female, and just as obviously being very careful not to precipitate any kind of trouble with Sage. Here I was alongside five grizzlies, but unable to get a picture due to the heavy cover and a desire to keep myself out of trouble. The younger male was constantly on the move in a very erratic manner.

While I was wondering what to do next, the female resolved the problem for me by getting to her feet and leading a whole parade of grizzlies up a cow trail toward the summit of a butte, the smaller male bringing up the rear at a discreet distance.

The next few days gave us no glimpse of Sage and the female, although we saw the cubs and the younger male several times. It was June, the mating time for grizzlies, and undoubtedly Sage and his new-found mate had wandered off by themselves on a kind of ursine honeymoon.

Who can say what really motivates any kind of life to choose a certain path? Sage had come to the ranch from the mountains years before, and he regularly returned to them when the spirit moved him. Except for mating time, he was always alone and very secretive. For the most part he was like a ghost bear, an almost intangible presence that we knew about but saw very rarely.

One hot summer afternoon I was fishing for trout on Cottonwood Creek, where it winds down through our ranch meadows, when a thunderstorm rolled down from the western peaks. One minute the sun was shining, beating down in oppressive heat, and the next it was pouring rain. Taking shelter under a big spreading willow, I watched javelins of lightning shooting down here and there accompanied by blasts of thunder that rolled and reverberated among the mountains.

When the storm passed, the air was fresh and delightfully cool as I walked past a big aspen grove toward some beaver dams upstream. A shaft of sun broke through the dispersing clouds to light up a green, flower-spangled meadow as I came around a point of trees. Standing in the middle of it, like some pagan god, was a mighty grizzly. For a long moment, he stood — a bronze statue, huge, rugged and the picture of power. Then he turned and loped away into the thick cover of some willows at the edge of a swamp. It was the last time I would see Sage.

That fall we found his tracks in new snow where he had crossed the meadows not far from that same place — unmistakable marks with those two bent toes on his right front paw — and they pointed towards the high country back among the peaks.

Where he dug his wintering den that year will always be a mystery. If it could be found, it would likely prove to be his grave.

The King Elk

Mist hung, thickly shrouding the big timberline larches around our camp as I saddled the night horse to round up the packstring that was feeding somewhere on the high meadows above. The late August air was damp and cool, with heavy dew clinging to everything along the trail that wound its way towards the summit of the Continental Divide, and there were no sounds except the creaking of saddle leather accompanying the soft blowing of my mount.

As we climbed, the mist began to thin out and brighten, and when we came to a saddle at the top of the ridge where the trail forked, we suddenly broke into bright sunlight. Reining the horse toward a shale-covered hump to one side, I stopped to listen. From somewhere below in the fog came the musical sound of the Swiss bells worn by some of the horses, and my saddle horse immediately pricked his ears, wanting to be off after them. But I checked him to enjoy a look at the panorama spread out in every direction.

The peaks poked sharp and clear from the gently undulating sea of mist that shone in the sun like old silver. From the edge of the prairies ten miles to the east, to the top of the McDonald Range fifty miles to the west, the mist hid everything below timberline. Only the tops of the mountains showed; familiar peaks, for I had climbed around and over most of them through the years, typical Rocky Mountain crags, each one with its own identifying profile, evoking memories of adventures past and a thousand campfires shared with those who chose to wander and live among the mountains.

Two hundred yards along the ridge on the edge of the mist, a movement caught my eye, the flash of antler tines in the sun, and a moment later a big bull elk walked out from behind a clump of shintangle scrub. I dismounted to sit under my horse's nose, and put my binoculars on the bull, as he climbed toward the ridge top. When he reached it, he stopped broadside as though he too wished to enjoy the view; a mighty bull, and when he turned his head, I recognized him.

In the hollow between his left shoulder and the base of his neck there was a silvery scar, contrasting sharply with his dark mane. Below the mark a distinctive wattle hung where a torn flap of skin had healed, a record of raking claws that had missed their hold. This one had a history. We called him King.

King's mother had been a herd leader; a big dominant cow whose size and willingness to guide a herd of close to a hundred females with calves and a scattering of yearling bulls, had won her that position. She was the one who broke trail through the deep snow in winter, chose the route and made the quick decisions when danger threatened. Leadership in such a herd is not won by fighting (although Old Buck's flashing front feet quickly punished any other cow daring to cross the invisible line of herd etiquette), but is a position which goes to the strong and the wise.

The individual animals of an elk herd display characters

ranging from timid to courageous, and a certain order of rank is always maintained. It is always a cow that is the trail boss. If one sees a herd going fast with a bull in the lead, it is likely an accident brought about by his efforts to escape danger with no thought for those that follow.

Elk are very gregarious animals. Except in spring, when the cows scatter far and wide to have their calves, the herds sometimes number in the hundreds. They gather into bunches in summer, and when the first deep snows of winter come, these consolidate into even bigger herds.

They feed in a definite pattern according to the season. From the higher country in summer, after the calves are big enough to travel, they go down to the ridges at the edge of the mountains for the winter. When the grass begins greening on the lower slopes and flats in spring, they move down for the fresh feed, and then work their way slowly back into high country to avoid summer's heat and flies.

So, in late March, Old Buck led her herd up over the pass out of Horseshoe Basin. She halted the herd at the summit, and for a while they stood outlined in a long rank against the snowy flanks of the mountain called the Horn. She had a choice of two trails descending the ridge — one a summer elk trail pitched at a steep angle across a shale slide, and the other, man-made, on an easier grade. Old Buck took neither of them, but cut across the north shoulder of the Horn where the winds had whipped the snow off, and down into the head of a big draw. From there she picked a trail along the south face to a bunch grass bench, and then on down to the park boundary near the head of Cottonwood Creek. At first starshine the herd came out in a long line onto a flat flanking a swamp by a big natural salt lick.

They were salt-hungry, and many of them began avidly licking the mud where alkali had leached out onto the surface while the rest fed on the new green grass. The moon came out from behind a bank of clouds to light up a pastoral

54

scene of primeval wildness. The whole flat was alive with the moving shapes of the great deer, and the night musical with their conversational squeals. As usual at this time of year, there were no mature bulls with the bunch, only a few two-year-olds, slab-sided and gaunt after the long winter, and still carrying their antlers.

Upon her arrival at the lick, Old Buck walked around the rest of the bunch, stopping here and there to listen and test the wind. It told of peace — a night belonging to the elk, full of stars with the soft, warm smell of spring everywhere. The balmy breeze played with the long hair of her mane, and her ears flickered as a coyote yapped, having discovered the herd. But she was not concerned about the little grey wolf. A great horned owl flew by on silent wings in quest of a snow-shoe hare or a mouse. Satisfied, she ambled back through the herd to lick at the salty mud, satisfying a craving for the minerals winter and the twin calves in her womb had drained from her body.

As spring progressed, the herd began to split up in search of fresh pastures, spending their days in indolent napping among the aspen groves, and coming out to feed when they were hungry. The young bulls went off by themselves and the yearlings, no longer encouraged by the cows to follow them, formed their own bunches. By late May the cows were scattered far and wide, each seeking her own private calving place. Well hidden in willow thickets and aspen groves, they began to drop their calves.

Old Buck sought out a willow patch along Cottonwood Creek, where early one morning her calves were born — reddish, light-spotted, gangling little creatures, that seemed all eyes, ears and spindly legs.

She licked them dry, thus quickening their struggle to get to their feet, and encouraged them to wobble their way to her flanks, where they poked their noses around, fumbling for her teats. When they fastened onto them, they sucked her udder dry, then folded up again to sleep. She left them there, slumbering in the sun-dappled shade, while she wandered out across a meadow nearby to feed hungrily.

This was her routine during those first days of the calves' lives, a vulnerable and dangerous time for them as it would be two weeks before their legs would strengthen enough to allow them to keep up to her. Old Buck was never very far away and continually on the look-out, but in spite of her constant vigilance, two coyotes surprised her one evening.

She would have missed them entirely had she not caught a fleeting glimpse of one ghosting past fifty yards away, and heading straight for where the calves were hidden. She ran, and finding a coyote within two jumps of her young, she charged, striking with her front feet. It dodged and streaked away as one of her flying hooves grazed its tail. She pursued it and, perhaps because she was so close to it, she followed it too far. The coyote's mate streaked in behind her and grabbed one of the calves, quickly tearing its throat before dragging it away.

Old Buck came storming back, a living picture of rage, her hair standing up on her neck, her mouth open and her ears hanging loosely down on each side of her jaws as she reared to strike. The coyote dropped the calf to streak through a heavy clump of willows where she could not follow, and she quickly turned back to her young. The male was lying still in his bed, his big liquid eyes full of fear, but his sister was feebly retching for breath as her blood ran out of a torn jugular.

For a while the old cow licked her as though trying to bring life back into the limp little body, all the while nervously moving around and stamping her feet as she stood with head thrown up watching for the coyotes. The smell of them was in her nose, along with that of fresh blood, urging her to move. She roused her remaining calf to his feet and led him away. As soon as she was gone, the coyotes came back to quickly tear their kill to pieces. Eating some and burying the rest, they each took a piece back to their pups at the den.

Three days later, Old Buck came whisker-close to losing her remaining calf. He was cached in a small aspen grove by some beaver dams while she fed a hundred yards directly downwind. When her belly was full, she lay down in a patch of cow parsnip to chew her cud, half dozing in the warm morning sun. Suddenly she was lifted to her feet by a noseful of the sour-sweet smell of bear. At the same moment she caught a glimpse of the animal heading through a stringer of low willow growth toward her calf. Letting out a ringing alarm bark, she charged.

The black bear was only a few steps from the calf when she arrived. Without a moment's hesitation she reared, coming down hard with her front feet in a lightning fast one-two that sledge-hammered squarely in the middle of the bear's back. The spine of a lesser animal would have been broken, but bears are incredibly tough, and this one rolled out from under her to swivel on his feet, chopping at her brisket with his teeth. A swinging paw lifted a wad of hair off her neck, and she gave a wild, whistling snort and slammed him over the bridge of the nose with a clubbing hoof, quick as a striking snake. Knocked down again, the bear bawled, got up, and swung on his heels to get away.

Another cow had heard Old Buck's alarm bark and the ensuing ruckus, and she came charging in to help. The bear, finding himself overwhelmed by two raging demons bent on pounding him into the ground, fled in a panic. Both cows came charging after him, striking at his rump every time they got close enough. The bear came to a beaver dam and hit the edge of it at a dead run while looking back past his shoulder, whereupon the muck and water tripped him up in a great splash. He somersaulted, skidded on his back, and then went completely under in deep water. When he surfaced, he struck out, swimming for the opposite side, came out of the water at a gallop and was swallowed by the forest.

The cows did not try to pursue him, but turned to go pacing back toward their calves with noses elevated and heads held high.

In a few weeks King was transformed into a little saddle-brown replica of a full-grown elk, still juvenile in his outline, but now fleet-footed and fully able to keep up to his mother in their world of timber and meadows amongst the folds of ridges and hills at the foot of the mountains. She joined a herd of about thirty cows, part of the larger one she wintered with, and they wandered from one choice spot to another in the good feed of this lower ground. Their old winter hair was now replaced by short summer coats of rich brown, sleek and shiny over new fat. Most of their feeding was in the cool of the evening, at night and in early morning, for the fly season was at its height. To avoid the insects, the elk spent the hot hours bedded down in the shade of heavy timber.

Now the danger from predators was lessened by the number of elk and the mobility of the young ones; any one of them could outrun a bear. No coyote, however hungry, was likely to risk trying for a calf when faced with thirty sets of keen eyes, ears and nostrils backed up by a formidable will-ingness to fight when threatened. The calves were rarely vulnerable, for they were not inclined to wander far from their mothers.

One evening while the herd was feeding on a grassy flat, a grizzly wandered out of the timber on the upwind side. Instantly every cow was paying close attention. The big silvertip did not have elk in mind, but was just following his nose. The cows bunched, with their calves crowding close to their flanks. When the rank smell of grizzly filled her nostrils, Old Buck blew her nose with a sudden sharp snort, and broke into a run to lead the bunch away across the flat and up a long slope to higher ground.

When they came to a fence, she took it in one long, easy bound and the rest of the cows did the same. The calves slithered under the wires. One bull calf belonging to a young cow with twins, misjudged his stride and caught the second wire full in the mouth. It slammed him back, knocking him off his feet. He was instantly up and jumped again. This time his front feet went between the second and third wires, and he somersaulted with the wires twisted around his legs, suspending him upside down. Squealing and thrashing, the calf struggled to get free, but the wire clung to him, a barb caught in the soft skin of a foreleg.

The calf's mother missed him when the herd stopped in a low saddle flanked by aspens a quarter-mile beyond. But her remaining calf began to suckle, lulling her first impulse to go back, and by the time it was finished, the herd was on the move again. She was nervous, but out of long habit she went with it, leaving the trapped one.

By daylight, the calf was nearly dead. Shortly, a coyote found him, quickly cut the remaining threads of life, and howled a message to its mate — news of a juicy windfall.

King, fed by his mother's rich milk and now without competition in the suckling, grew fast. Like the other calves, he quickly learned to eat the variety of herbage in abundance everywhere. From the beginning, he showed a strong tendency to dominate the other calves as they played.

Regularly every evening and early morning, while the herd was grazing, the calves would explode in play. While much of the time it was a disorganized racing in all directions, it sometimes followed a pattern. One evening, by accident or design, the calves lined up in a circle that took them single file around the bunched cows in a flat-out gallop. Seeming to be caught in the excitement most of the cows lifted their heads to watch. Two of them towered straight up on their hind feet, their noses elevated to the maximum and their briskets touching as they pawed at each other. They shouldered into each other as they came down, then made a full turn and sashayed off to the side to break the ring of running calves, first one cow running ahead of her partner to check her with a shouldering motion, and then the other repeating the manoeuvre. Other cows paired off in similar frolic until the whole flat was a mix-up of playing animals. Then, suddenly, they all stopped and stood still for a while before resuming their feeding.

Another day, early in the morning, they came down to a pond among some low hills to drink. The little lake was shallow and, like a circular mirror, reflected a long line of drinking elk cows standing shoulder to shoulder, their images in detailed duplicate on the surface. King suddenly shyed in mock fright at his own reflection, jumped into the water, leapt back on shore and then in again. A moment later half-a-dozen calves had joined him, shattering their reflections as they threw water in all directions. A cow and a young bull with first-year spikes in velvet raced out into the pond, bucking and plunging, pawing and whirling in a wild pas de deux that threw sparkling sheets of water high in the air. The rest of the bunch stood like spectators on the edge of an arena.

Ever-vigilant, Old Buck was standing up the slope behind the herd, when she spotted the rider sitting on his horse in a dip between two knolls across the lake. Her alarm bark stopped the play instantly, every elk frozen where it stood. King came running to his mother, and as if that was the signal, the whole herd went streaming away out of sight.

The wavelets of the little lake subsided, the sharp reflections of the mountains took shape again in the mirror stillness. I was left alone with my horse in the wings of a natural amphitheatre, the recent scene of wild action and great beauty.

Outside the breeding season most of the bulls range in small bunches by themselves, and during the summer months, the growing, velvet-covered antlers are tender and vulnerable to flies. So the bulls spend a large part of their time feeding and loafing along the open slopes above and around timberline. By August, their new antlers are fully grown, the velvet beginning to dry, and an uncomfortable itching sets in around their bases. The bulls rub them on saplings and clumps of brush, stripping off the remaining velvet in long, bloody rags, For a few days the newly uncovered antlers are ugly with splotches of dried blood on their bone-white surfaces, but this is soon changed by much vigorous rubbing against trees. The colour of the antlers is shaded by the kind of growth used by the bulls for the polishing. Aspen or cottonwood stains the antler beams and points a rich tan shade, and willows make them a bit darker. The bulls that polished their headgear on alders had weapons stained a rich mahogany brown. In contrast the points gleamed like polished ivory from being repeatedly thrust into the ground.

In mid-August, the proportion of light to dark hours changes as the earth turns toward the winter months, and this brings about a very subtle and delicate hormonal change in the bulls' body chemistry. Their testes enlarge and their summer passivity begins to be replaced by a desire for competition with each other. A certain hierarchy is estab-lished between individuals, a prelude to the coming rut. This change prompts no extra movement or effort on the part of the cows; their procreative organs are primed for the coming estrus of the breeding season.

By September Old Buck's bunch had worked its way gradually up among the mountains and the rut was in full swing. She was still the trail boss when the group was on the move, but her females were now in the harem of a mighty bull with a heavy rack of antlers — seven points to a side. The beams curved out from his head and then swept gracefully back toward his rump; mighty weapons, polished, hard and sharp. Because Old Buck was inclined to lead out for new ground under the pressure of his herding, she was sometimes roughly prodded back into the herd. King was nervous when this great grunting and whistling male came close, but he was only a spectator in this first mating moon.

The mountain slopes rang with the bugling of the bulls as they challenged each other for dominance over the harems of cows. Each herdmaster's rivals were continually trying to cut out females for themselves. Most of the competing was done by manoeuvring, displaying great antlers and bugling; all these maintained the social pecking order among the bulls. At times, however, when a lesser one pressed too close, there would be a quick charge by the ruling bull and almost invariably the usurper would give way, fleeing to avoid a clash.

Individual character among the males ranged from the awkward and unsure advances of the novices to the paramount arrogance displayed by the dominant herdmasters. Some of the bulls, regardless of age, were naturally timid. While these might make a great deal of noise, a few would go for years without knowing the surging passion of covering a cow.

Because of the size of the harem he ruled, the herdmaster of Old Buck's bunch was almost continually harried by questing bulls bent on cutting cows out of his herd. His resting and feeding periods were fleeting. When he was not driving away a rival, he was herding, following individual cows and continually testing the ripening of their estrus period until they stood still to be mounted. His outline grew gaunt, his eyes took on an almost insane gleam of passion and he reeked of urine and musk. He was an animal driven, a pawn of the game being played under the mating moon.

By the time the mating season had waned, he was slab-sided, thin and almost tottering with exhaustion, and he went off alone to seek some rest and feed to build up his body for the long, hard months of the winter ahead.

Although she was fat and vigorous, Old Buck was not in calf. Age was beginning to tell on her and so she joined the ranks of the dry cows. But this did not diminish her qualities of leadership; she was still the accepted trail boss and once more in full charge of her bunch. It had been joined by others and now included about a hundred cows, fifty calves and a scattering of adolescent bulls.

Compared to their weight of a few pounds at birth, the calves had grown apace, averaging about a two-pounds-a-day weight gain throughout the first months of their lives. Still their mothers suckled and guarded them; they were less vulnerable to predators, but the risk was not entirely gone.

In late Indian summer, when the days were sparkling clear, the nights frosty and the air had a tang of autumn, King was lying asleep a few yards upslope from his dozing mother on the edge of the herd, when a big lynx crawled onto a boulder slightly above and downwind of him. Its fur matched the grey of the rock, so that the cat was almost invisible as it crouched, looking through keen, cold, yellow eyes down across the mountain meadow, where the herd was bedded down.

Directly in front of the hungry cat, the flicking of an ear gave away King's position, just a bound or two beyond a patch of low, shintangle pines. The lynx sagged back, stepping down off the rock and slinking like a shadow into the tangled mat of the scrub. Not a twig snapped as it stalked. The cat came to the edge of the cover, gathering itself for its final leap onto the sleeping calf, when a squirrel feeding on the fat cones on top of a nearby pine spotted him, and cut loose in a sudden tirade of chattering.

Things happened fast. Old Buck jerked her head up at the instant the lynx launched itself. The sudden noise had thrown its timing off just the width of a hair, and as King came up on his feet, claws as sharp as razors dug into his back and neck while the cat's teeth closed on the skin on one side of his neck near the forward slope of his shoulder.

The calf bawled in surprise and pain as he and the lynx rolled over in a tangle of squirming limbs. The next instant Old Buck boiled into the mix-up with a sharp snort of rage. A driving front foot came down on the lynx's back and skidded off to pin down a hind leg. The cat squalled and released its intended victim, who rolled out between his mother's spraddled hind legs. Ears dropping and eyes bulging with anger and intent to kill, the cow reared again to trample the lynx, but it dodged her stabbing hoofs to roll sideways and come up at a scrambling run for cover. Old Buck pursued closely, but again the lynx dodged, jumping for a scraggly aspen growing out of some rocks. A broken hind leg threw it off balance and it fell back to the ground. Before it could gather itself up, the cow was all over it, tramping it savagely until it was only a sodden, bloody rag of fur.

When she turned back to her calf, she found him bleeding profusely. A flap of skin was torn loose from his neck and hung down, raw side out, under an exposed piece of raw flesh. It was a sore wound but not deep, although it was bleeding profusely. King nuzzled his mother and trembled while she licked him, as they stood surrounded by excited cows sniffing the blood and the dead lynx.

The wound soon stopped bleeding, but for several days it was raw and sore. When it began to heal, it contracted and the hanging flap of skin shrunk into a slightly pendulous wattle. Meanwhile ravens eyed the calf with anticipation and magpies hovered close, ready to share the windfall of misfortune. Coyotes smelled blood and hung around the outskirts of the herd. But Old Buck was vigilant day and night and kept King close to her.

When the wound finally closed, it made a distinctive

mark that King would wear the rest of his life. At first the wattle was topped by a patch of bare skin, but gradually whitish hair grew over it, making the brand even more distinctive.

At three years old, King was a big elk, wearing new antlers that were exceptionally heavy, with four well developed tines on each side. He summered high in the mountains with a small bunch of bulls, sharing feed that was nothing less than exotic in its lushness and brilliance of bloom. As the first stirrings of the rut stimulated the bulls, he joined in the preliminary sparring and shoving with such arrogance and gusto that older bulls were sometimes pressed close to an outright fight.

By the time the rutting season arrived his neck muscles were thick and heavy, his whole body tuned to toughness, and his strength honed to a fine edge by the exercise. It was the third rut of his life and the first in which he would take active part, although young bulls rarely have the opportunity to breed.

That fall I was guiding a professional photographer out to make a film featuring wildlife in the mountains. We were camped in the park among the elk there, taking advantage of every hour of good light to record the rut as part of his motion picture. Drama and excitement unfolded in almost every direction at all hours of the day and night, for the breeding season of the elk was in full swing, and the mountains rang with the bugling of the bulls. We enjoyed those golden moments when everything was right; there was action aplenty, and my friend was beside himself with excitement as he exposed film of the elk playing their roles out among golden aspens and evergreens against the backdrop of peaks. And sometimes we were keenly disappointed by being out of range when something dramatic happened, or when the light went bad.

One afternoon we sat on the edge of a meadow in a

stringer of low brush listening to the bulls tune up after a lull in the middle of an unusually hot day. Most of the elk were in the timber, the males sounding off with their various bugles ranging all the way from thin high-pitched squeals to deep pipe organ notes — the music of the bulls on the quest for cows, throwing their challenges back and forth full of wild and primitive lust.

Out of sight in the timber below us, two bulls were working their way down opposite slopes. Although they were completely hidden, we could locate them by their bugles. One appeared on the far edge of the open grassy bottom; a moment later the other walked into view directly across from him. Both were lesser, unattached bulls, the kind that continually harry the herdmasters. There were no cows to fight over, the bulls were coming together for no other reason than excitement and anger at each other's presence.

As they closed the gap between them, stalking along with heads held low, my friend began shooting film. He should have waited, for he was rewinding his camera when they collided. The collision wasn't violent, they just walked into each other like two animated mechanical things going in opposite directions on the same track. After the first clash, they stood braced, testing each other, their antlers banging and rattling as they manoeuvred for position.

Again the camera began to whir, but suddenly it stopped and the photographer began muttering words he never learned in church, as he struggled to clear the jammed film. While he worked frantically, the bulls put on a show that couldn't have been better if they had been directed. Their movements put them into a wash of bare earth along a water-course where their footwork churned up the dust, all backlit dramatically in the lowering sun. Just as the camera began running again, they suddenly stopped and looked at each other as though mutually surprised at this profligate waste of energy. Then one went back into the timber and the other

66

went up the wash to a place where all but his back and antlers were hidden. There he began horning a steep cutbank, stirring up a cloud of dust. The photographer sat looking on in absolute disgust, punctuating his feelings by spitting into the grass at his boot toes with a fervour of silent frustration that went beyond the expression of his vocabulary.

Above us a big bull with a small harem of cows appeared on a bare, steep hogback ridge running down into the valley. Behind him we could hear another bull. When this one appeared, I recognized him by the silvery scar in the hollow of his shoulder. He circled onto the ridge above the herdmaster, challenging him bugle for bugle, while the older bull stood facing him. Suddenly the young bull charged like a streak of light. Horns rattled sharply as the elk tangled. The attack must have taken the older animal by surprise, for before he could set himself, he was being propelled backwards down the steep slope through a tangle of low, snow-and-wind-twisted aspens. By the time he got his feet set and recovered his balance, they had gone over fifty yards. But age and experience showed as the herdmaster then sidestepped, parried the other's weapons and raked his flank with a fast slash that lifted hair off his hide. As suddenly as it had started, the fight broke off; the brash youngster retreating and disappearing into thick green timber.

We had watched another dramatic encounter, this time out of camera range, and I was beginning to feel sorry for my friend.

As we mounted our horses to head for camp, a shower blew in from the west, soaking everything, but by the time we reached the top of the ridge it was clearing. Vagrant, fluffy wafers of mist hung here and there on the mountain flanks, and the setting sun lit up the sky overhead.

My friend had just set up his camera to record this scene, when a huge old bull with his cows appeared out of the timber directly below us. Leaving our horses, we sneaked down through some scrub to a spot within a hundred yards of the bunch, and suddenly four more bulls appeared out of nowhere, almost walking over us. They passed us in single file circling the bunch in front.

Putting my call to my mouth, I almost lifted my friend bodily off the ground as I let out a bugle beside his ear, hoping to stir up some action. Instantly, the passing bulls stopped to answer, and their ringing challenges echoed off the mountain slopes. The big herd boss stalked toward us, his nose thrust out and his magnificent antlers laid back along his flanks as he blew a long column of vapour from his open month, the prelude to a bell-like sound that resembled water being poured from a huge glass jug. This musical call was followed by a deep-toned bugle that had power, savagery and an almost frightening quality of utter wildness in it.

The photographer beside me muttered with a fervour that was monumental, "Damn! There isn't enough light!"

There was a movement among some spruces on the far side of the herd as a young bull came into view, and I was astonished to recognize King. Without uttering a sound, he sneaked through a patch of small trees, going straight toward a cow as though drawn by a string fastened to his nose. And to my further astonishment, she stood perfectly still as he reared and mounted her. He fumbled a bit in his steaming excitement, but then penetrated her, thrusting hard in a straining plunge just as the old bull spotted him and charged. Before the outraged harem boss could reach him, King had disengaged and whirled away. He was an enterprising and energetic bull, this one, an individual of character marked by more than his identifying scar.

The photographer sat beside me watching him go, repeatedly pounding the ground with his fist. Stalking elk with a camera that day had been heavily laced with both excitement and disappointment; long on action and short on success; the vagaries of the game sometimes taxing a man's patience to the breaking point.

The following winter was a hard one with deep snow. Old Buck's herd had a new leader, for the old cow had taken a hunter's bullet through the fleshy part of a ham the previous fall, and though the wound had healed, she was lame. Her face was grey with age, and the prolonged cold weather had worn her down till her bones showed through her faded buckskin coat. But somehow she stuck to the herd, though hard pressed at times to keep up, as they trailed through the deep snow from one feeding area to another.

The season was cruel with heavy drifts and a sharp crust on the snow. As usual, the mule deer suffered most, the coyotes taking them almost at will, for they were weak and vulnerable. The sheep were cut down in numbers too, though not as much. The coyotes left the elk pretty much alone, although any animal that was weakened by age or infirmity was usually quickly found and literally eaten alive. Most of the casualties among the elk were older bulls caught by the early storms before they had had time to recover from the rut. By spring there were very few of these left.

King was ranging with his mother's herd on the wind-whipped slopes stretching from the mouth of Pine Creek to the long open mountain side above Indian Springs, a piece of country stretching over several miles. Like most of his age group, he was gaunt but strong when I saw him pawing for feed over the winter months. He was the biggest bull accompanying the herd that winter, easily identifiable among the cows and a scattering of other young bulls.

The hard weather broke in mid-March and a warm chinook wind melted the snow until only the biggest drifts showed, greyish white in contrast to the new green grass on the hills and flats of lower ground. As usual, Old Buck's bunch left the park about this time, climbing over the pass out of Horseshoe Basin in a long, slow-travelling, straggling line. Far in the rear, Old Buck hobbled slowly along, favouring her stiffened leg, and by the time she crested the ridge, the rest of the herd was out of sight among the folds of timber below.

She stood on the skyline, resting, every line of her frame spelling fatigue, before she began picking her way down the track. At the rim of a steep-sided draw, where the herd had slid down on thawing ground, she half fell on the poor footing and hurt her injured leg. Again she stood still for a while on a hard-packed drift that bridged a small stream, smelling the track where it climbed through some willows on the opposite side. Under her feet, she heard the muted rattling of the little creek as it poured through a tunnel cut through the snow. Ahead of her was the steep pitch, while below her the hard-packed crust offered an inviting alternative toward lower ground. Accepting the invitation she began picking her way down the easier route, till she came to a narrow cleft where the draw's sides pinched in between steep banks, offering no choice of way. She had no means of knowing that the creek had thinned the crust here, until suddenly she broke through and found her feet in rushing water and snow almost level with her back. She was trapped, and she seemed to accept her fate without a struggle. That night she died. Under a canopy of stars, with the smell of green meadows on the warm breeze — meadows she would never see again — life left her in one long sigh.

At sunrise, a great grizzly, following his nose upwind, hungry for feed after an early exit from his winter den, appeared over the edge of the draw above the dead elk. He went straight to the carcass, grabbed it by the neck with his teeth and heaved it out of the hole as effortlessly as a terrier would handle a rabbit. Backing up the steep slope, he

70

dragged Old Buck's body into a thicket where pussy willows hung soft and silvery, and tore it open.

When the big bear left the vicinity a few days later, there was nothing left of the elk but a mat of loose hair, the skull and a few of the larger bones. The grizzly's mounds of dung, thick with the hair he had eaten with the meat, were all deposited in a shallow hollow nearby, where the waxy-green pointed leaves of glacier lilies broke through the leaf mould reaching for the sun. Like every other living thing in the mountains, the old cow had sprung from the soil, grown to full maturity, raised calves that now propagated her kind themselves, and had returned to the earth. The cycle was complete.

Following that winter, King disappeared. Every time I saw elk, I looked for him, but he had completely vanished. It was as though he, too, had been swallowed by the earth, and I decided that a cougar or a hunter had got him. But I kept looking for a bull with a wattle topped by a silvery scar on the base of his neck.

One day I was riding the skyline along the crest of the Continental Divide. On the far side of a big basin near the headwaters of a wilderness creek which ran southwest toward the Flathead River and the Pacific Ocean, I spotted four bull elk. They were lying partially concealed in some timberline scrub, and when I focused the binoculars on them, it was obvious that the biggest one had spotted me. Half a mile away, he stood up and walked out onto a little promontory where he stood broadside with his eyes fixed in my direction.

Even at that range, his antlers evoked a gasp of admiration — eight fully developed points to a side, heavy in the beams, wide in spread with beautiful double-curved symmetry.

For a while he stood as motionless as a bronze statue, looking my way, then he swung his head a little and I thought I caught a silvery flash at the base of his neck on the left side. Could it be King? My excitement suddenly towered, and I longed for the powerful spotting scope forgotten back in camp. His three companions all stood up to join him, aware of his interest, and one by one their eyes fastened on my horse and me where we stood silhouetted against the blue sky. Finally, they began moving away in single file up a saddle to drop from sight over the skyline. I pursued them through the timber in the bottom of the basin and up the other side. Before reaching the top, I tied my horse in a clump of trees and climbed on foot to a point overlooking the country beyond.

From there I was looking down into a tangle of logs, with second growth and the bone-white, bleached-out spikes of old fire-killed trees still standing. There was no sign of the bulls at first, but then my glasses picked up a spot of colour that might have been the tan hide of an elk among some alders far down in the steep bottom of a draw. For a long while there was no movement, and then, a little beyond, the glasses caught a glint of something, and I made out the gleaming antler tines of a bull.

Slipping back over the skyline, I circled under the crest of a spur to get the wind in my favour, and then I climbed down toward the elk, making use of every contour and cover. At last, I came out over the ravine on a knob directly above where I had last seen the bulls, and sat down behind a log.

Not a whisker of them was in sight; they had again vanished completely and my disappointment was keen. The powerful lenses of the binoculars minutely combed every detail of the surrounding slopes without revealing a sign of them.

Picking up a dead branch lying beside me, I rattled it sharply against a little dead tree. Like magic, antlers began to rise up from the brush, as the bulls got out of their beds. Three of them were mighty animals, two with six points to a

72

side and one with seven, all grand bulls; but the fourth one was magnificent.

His brow tines swung down and curved up almost even with the end of his nose. The bez and trez tines were heavy and long. His top royals were massive, fully two feet in length, their tips gleaming like two upright ivory spears. Back of these along the main beams were four more fully developed points with the last two forking deeply. When he first stood up his rump was toward me, but when he turned, there on his neck was the familiar mark. I had found King again and he was truly an imperial bull.

A week later I saw him on the crest of the Divide standing in the sunshine over valleys filled with fog. He had changed his territory, crossing two ranges of mountains, and was now located in some of the most remote wilderness in the British Columbia Rockies. He was in the heart of my packtrain outfitting country, so when I headed out with a string of twenty horses and a photographer friend from New York a couple of weeks later, it was with the express purpose of finding and filming King.

My guest was Sheridan St. John, one of the earliest television producers to specialize in nature films, and an internationally famous outdoor sports writer. Like all his kind, he combined business with pleasure, so this expedition with his cameras was also a holiday. To make it even more pleasurable we were good friends.

There is something intangible about the companionship enjoyed by two people far removed in their choices of environment, yet close in their common interests and outlook on life. My companion was an old hand at this game — although he spent most of his time in the concrete and steel canyons of the big city, he was passionately fond of getting out into wild country and had been on expeditions into remote parts of the world.

Around many campfires over several years we had traded

stories of our experiences. He could tell of stalking oryx, guided by a Bushman tracker in the searing heat of the African desert, or of the high adventure of filming Inuit as they hunted polar bears on the limitless sea ice of the Arctic.

From the snug camp we set up on this trip, we spent our days wandering on horseback along rugged horizons, dipping into timberline basins set like green jewels among the high jagged peaks. As always it was more demanding and much more difficult than ordinary hunting, for the photographer depends upon good light to record the drama and magic on the emulsion of colour film. It has its advantages too, for the trophies are brought back on film with no bag limits or closed seasons, and one need never worry about the boundaries of areas closed to hunting with guns. This was early September and all the big bulls had their harems collected: the cliffs rang with their bugling.

Early one morning, after we had been out for several days, we were riding through an old burn in rough country along a divide between two minor watersheds, a place heavily cut by deep ravines full of second growth timber, and mountain meadows. It was slow going and after several miles, we had not seen an elk although their sign was everywhere. At noon we rode out on a rim overlooking a deep box canyon, which opened out below us into a heavily timbered valley.

Tieing our horses out of sight, we walked out to a point to eat lunch and use our glasses. At first we could see nothing, a situation not necessarily indicating an absence of elk, for there was enough cover in this broken-up place to hide a sizable herd. When my binoculars were trained on the slope directly opposite, a light coloured spot showed up at the foot of a big old spruce in an island of mature timber the fire had missed. A look through the twenty-power spotting scope revealed a sleek cow lying half asleep chewing her cud in the shade beneath an overhanging alder.

At a range close to half a mile it was like unravelling the design of a picture puzzle wherein hidden figures lie; one after another six more cows took form with only parts of them visible.

Then up near the top of a strip of thick growing alder brush, a spike bull stood up in plain view and gave an adolescent squeal. A hundred yards below him, directly above the cows, a huge bull came to his feet, only his head and neck in sight, and bugled back, then twisted his antlers into the brush, savaging the alder bark and making the leaves fly. There was no mistaking those massive antlers. It was King.

Sheridan whistled softly through his teeth at the sight of him. Here was a leading character in an elk movie — the biggest bull either one of us had ever seen.

To try to get within camera range in that jungle was impossible even without the capricious mountain air currents to give away our location, so we just waited to see where the elk would go when they got up to feed.

Following the flurry of bugling and momentary excitement both bulls lay down again, and for a long while nothing happened. Then, as the sun began to dip towards the skyline, the first cow I had spotted got to her feet and began nibbling at a low bush. More cows got up and began to move around, and the spike bull squealed. Instantly the whole valley came alive with the music of rutting bulls; the place was alive with them. When the cows began to move up valley it was time for us to start our stalk.

We headed down the slope of the canyon through a heavy stand of second-growth lodgepole pine, slipping between their trunks and around and over a clutter of dead logs. We came out on top of a low cliff and climbed down onto the bench below. It was hot and still as we found a way through more timber and the sweat was running off us. We came out on the rim of another cliff a hundred yards above the creek, directly across from two open strips of grass, uprooted trees and scattered boulders separated by a stringer of green timber — avalanche tracks. They would give the camera good play; the kind of set-up a photographer looks for. Down the valley at least a half dozen bulls were sounding off.

Sheridan set up his loaded camera on its tripod and we waited. It is one thing to sit still in the mountain quiet, and quite another to do so while listening to a wild symphony coming closer and closer — a concert as primitive as the sight of midnight stars reflected on the mirror surface of a rock-bound lake.

I slipped around a clump of brush for a better view down valley and then a twisting thermal of wind went by, blowing the wrong way. I held my breath, for which way the elk would go would depend on how that puff of air current delivered our scent. The sharp alarm bark of a cow suddenly silenced the concert.

The timber cracked directly below and there was the tan flash of a cow jumping a log as she headed up the valley. She was followed by several more cows, and then King went by at a gallop, his nose outthrust and his great antlers laid back as he cleared the log at a long bound.

Stepping back, I murmured, "Look sharp! Here they come!"

Timber was snapping and cracking all over the slope as elk burst into view on the grass strips; bulls, cows and calves all going at a dead run like a cavalcade of steeple chasers. King was running behind a string of cows low down the slope — a magnificent sight as he galloped over the rough ground.

They milled around for a minute or two at the base of the cliff before doubling back and coming down the canyon directly opposite us. There were fifty-three cows and calves, four big bulls and three smaller bulls. King stopped on the skyline, outlined against a white cloud, every detail of him dramatically lit up by the lowering sun. Then he was gone.

"Holy smoke!" Sheridan muttered, letting out a long breath, "What a bull! That's the best shot I ever got of elk on the move." Then he added, "Can we find that bull again? I want some more footage of him."

"It won't be easy," I told him. "It's a big country, but maybe we'll be lucky."

We were lucky. We found King and his harem again in the middle of a grove of big western larches. The giant timber, some of the reddish brown trunks four feet in diameter, soared aloft for eighty to a hundred feet before spreading out in a broken canopy of foliage, all golden with autumn. It was remarkably like a well-tended park, with very little undergrowth and few downed logs, so we could see for two or three hundred yards in places. The golden rays of sunlight filtering through the foliage lit up the forest floor like something out of an artist's dream.

Quietly moving against the wind as close as we dared to the herd, we could see the elk scattered among the trees, some lying down and some feeding. Standing out among them was King.

Spreading the legs of the camera tripod on top of a low knoll behind a screening salmon berry bush, Sheridan began recording a wild and utterly beautiful mountain scene. It was early afternoon, and a lull in the rutting activity brought relatively placid interaction between individuals of the herd. King was the only bull in sight, though there had to be others close by.

After Sheridan had rolled considerable film of the scene before us, he murmured, "If that big character would stir himself to do something spectacular, it would be perfect."

I knew there was a good chance of blowing the whole herd out of sight by calling in a second bull, but thinking it was worth the risk, I took out my call. Pulling in a chest full of mountain air, I cut loose with a challenge.

Instantly King swung around to face us, and pointing his nose directly at us, he let out a short bugle that sounded deceptively like an immature bull. Then he stalked deliberately toward us, his nose outthrust and his massive horns swinging in cadence with his stride. I kept quiet; nothing is worse than overdoing the calling. Closer and closer he came, an awesome sight moving in and out of patches of shade over the yellowing grass, a power and majesty beyond words about him. Thirty steps from us he stopped, his front feet planted on a little mound where a tree had been uprooted long ago. His nose lifted as he opened his mouth to bugle right in our faces.

His head suddenly swung around, and looking in the direction he pointed, I saw another big bull coming toward us. This one had us in plain view. We froze, hoping he wouldn't spot us, but it was too late. For a long moment the second bull stood with his head high and his eyes pinned on us, then he swung on his heels to leave at a tearing run.

For a few seconds flashes of elk showed between trees as the herd stampeded away, then we were all alone.

Sheridan straightened, exclaiming, "That was something to see! But sure as hell this would be a poor place for a man with a weak heart!"

The weather held good and for the next week we rambled far and wide trying to pick up King and his harem again. They seemed to have evaporated into the mountain air.

One night it clouded up and began to snow. In the morning our tents sagged under the weight, and more was coming down. It was time to leave, for our grub was running low and Sheridan was due at a meeting in New York in a few days, so we packed up our gear and headed out. Breaking trail over a high pass that afternoon, the horses strung out behind me plodding through a driving blizzard, the trees beside the trail burdened under heavy loads of snow, it was hard to believe that only the day before we had ridden for hours in the warm sun dressed only in blue jeans and shirts.

This was the prelude to one of the toughest winters the country had ever seen. In late October, King and eleven other mature bulls settled on a south-facing slope on a ridge running west from the Continental Divide. The place was open to the sun with a heavy growth of cured bunch grass to give them good feed through the deep snows of winter.

By December the snow was as deep as it usually ever gets. At Christmas time, the temperature dropped to forty below and it stayed cold without a break. No crust impeded the bulls pawing for food, but the snow continued to build up. By late January they were wallowing half-way up to their ribs in snow, and finding it hard to get enough to eat. They were within sight of a cabin in the valley bottom, and the trapper who lived there often watched them.

One frosty morning in February, he was fastening his snowshoe harness as he got ready to leave for a day on his trapline. He was surprised to see the bulls coming along the trail leading past his cabin ploughing their way down the valley. They passed not more than fifty yards away, their antlers swinging, steam shooting from their noses with the exertion, and their coats rimed silvery with frost. Their ribs showed, and short rations had dulled their usual caution to the point of paying him little attention, but they were still going strong.

A half-mile below his cabin, where the trail comes close to the creek, there is a long stretch of open water where big springs keep the ice from forming. Here the bulls took to the easier going of water travel, and proceeded to fill up on the browse overhanging the stream. They then bedded down in the deep snow along the top of the low bank.

It was a welcome break for them but also a trap. The snow got deeper and deeper until it was over six feet on the level, so by the time the willow browse within reach began to thin out, the bulls' movements were restricted to the half-mile stretch of open water. The cold continued and as the bulls foraged, the splashes their feet threw up froze on the hair of their bellies and sides. The cold armour that only warm weather could remove quickly grew thicker and heavier. The fast-diminishing feed coupled with this extra weight cruelly drained their remaining strength.

The following spring I met the trapper one day in town, and he told me about it. "They must have been carrying over a hundred pounds of ice apiece," he said. "And they ate everything off till there wasn't a twig along that creek any smaller than your thumb. They got so weak, they couldn't take it any more. They would crawl up in the snow to lay down for the night and in the morning they just couldn't get up. One by one they died. I've never seen anything like it. It sure was one hell of a winter for the animals!"

In early summer I had a fishing party out in that valley, and I took some time to look for King's remains. Searching through the brush alongside the creek, I found what was left of eleven of the bulls — just scraps of hair, antlers and bones scattered by bears. But in spite of searching back and forth for hours there was no sign of King.

Had he somehow managed to save enough strength to move to better feed and survive? I stood in a little meadow within a few yards of the cheerfully chattering stream, and wondered if somewhere high on the slopes he knew so well, he lay in the warm sun basking among brilliant flowers. It was highly unlikely, for nobody ever saw the great bull with the silvery blaze on his neck again, but it was heart-warming to think that among the survivors of that terrible winter, there were undoubtedly some of his sons and daughters.

While he and Buck have long gone, somewhere among the valleys walk other bulls and cows, maintaining that bloodline and ensuring that each fall, when the first frost touches the mountain slopes, there will be wild music and action in the land of the elk.

Misty

It was the first cold snap of early winter, when the cold breath of the Arctic touches the rolling hills at the foot of the Rockies. The grass was ripe yellow and the willows and aspens bare of leaves, their naked branches and twigs etched against the sky in an intricate filigree of design, the buds sheathed against the frost and waiting for the warmth of the spring sun.

Overhead, high against the blue of the sky, the last of the migrating geese and ducks were winging south in honking, undulating Vs. They were not stopping, for the lakes and sloughs were covered by mirrors of hard, new ice. The bears were in their winter dens and everything else wearing hair and fur was fat, with a thick, heavy coat. The songbirds were long gone, leaving behind the woodpeckers, magpies, jays and chickadees now breaking the quiet of the aspen groves with cheerful calls.

The nights had been frosty and the days bright, the lingering warmth fading on the heels of a golden Indian summer. The morning sun had burned off the night's blanket of fog and now it lit up a jewelled world, where every blade of grass and every twig was decorated with glittering frost crystals under a spotless sky.

Jim Camp, a naturalist, climbed a hill not far from his home, and sat down at the base of a gnarled white pine to let his binoculars roam. The high, querulous honking of geese came to his ears, and the lenses of the powerful glasses picked up the flashing wings of a long V of late-migrating snow geese flying over a mile high. From where they had come, there was no telling, but they would not stop till far southwest of the Continental Divide. Behind them and considerably lower came a flock of greenhead mallards heading the same way. They were trailed by a small bunch of golden-eyes flying low, their fast-beating wings making a distinctive whistling sound. These would likely stop at the first open water on the river to loaf and feed a while before making the jump over the Rockies.

A movement on the edge of a meadow caught the naturalist's eye. The binoculars revealed a whitetail doe walking out through a stringer of low brush. When she came to the open meadow, she broke into a trot, heading for the sheltering timber on the other side. She was trailed by a pair of fawns and then a buck with heavy antlers, each one following exactly the same procedure as they crossed the meadow.

Again the glasses rambled, this time coming to rest focused on the flank of a mountain ridge two miles away. Black against a dusting of new snow, a band of bighorns moved erratically, as a ram stirred the bunch in the familiar routine of the rutting season. They were too far away for him to see horns, but the heavier, square outline of the ram revealed his identity to Jim's practiced eyes, for he had observed this ritual many times.

He got to his feet to walk down the slope. On a small bench, the frost was knocked off the grass, a line of tan showing plainly where an animal had crossed the side of the

82

hill. At first glance he thought it was the track of a deer, but when he bent over to examine it closely, he saw that it was the trail of a coyote.

He straightened up, letting out a soft whistle between his teeth. For a long time in this area coyote signs had been almost non-existent, but lately some had been showing up. The howl of a coyote was something he never heard any more, and he missed their choruses among the hills. A heavy and prolonged poison campaign had almost wiped them out, but now he was sure the coyotes were beginning to learn about poison.

When he thought of the lethal, odourless and tasteless stuff commonly called 1080, his jaw muscles bunched and his face took on grim lines. He had heartily hated the stuff ever since the county had first begun to use it years before, and he had come upon a coyote staggering in blind circles, stumbling and rising again in shuddering paroxysms of uncontrollable convulsions, with slaver drooling from its jaws. He had found a club and put the stricken animal out of misery, swearing to do something about the poison if it was the last thing he ever did. His determination became even more fixed when he found the carcass of a poisoned coyote partially eaten by birds, and a wide search through the trees around it revealed the scattered bodies of several chickadees and woodpeckers.

According to the company that made the poison and the county employees who mixed it in water to be injected into fresh horsemeat for coyote bait, this was impossible. Supposedly, birds could not eat enough to kill them. The baits were put out in cold weather that froze them solid. Coyotes could get enough to poison them, but birds couldn't. Either the people who made the stuff and those that used it didn't know all the facts, or they knew and didn't care, or, on the theory that if some was good more would be better, too much poison was being used in the baits.

The naturalist knew for sure that when the warm chinook winds blew, the baits thawed out and coyotes could eat a great deal more than it took to kill them. It was a well known fact that coyotes with just a tiny portion of poison in their systems could travel for many miles before dying. 1080 never killed instantly as did other poisons such as strychnine and cyanide, and its victims died slowly and in torture. If they ate a bellyful of the bait, they sometimes regurgitated part of it, and this in turn was poison that could be eaten by other animals. There was a strong doubt in Jim Camp's mind, that a sufficient amount of research had been done on the lethal qualities of the deadly stuff.

Camp had gone to the county council with his report, but they had only shrugged it off. His only consolation had been his belief that coyotes would learn to avoid the poison: now it looked like this was beginning to happen.

That same morning, something occurred on a ranch about twenty miles to the northeast that would have cheered him immensely had he seen it.

A handsome female coyote with an exceptionally fine silver-grey coat and a heavy brush, came out of a coulee with four fully grown pups trailing her. This was Misty; part of a generation of coyotes that ate nothing they had not killed, a product of the merciless poisoning campaign that had lasted fifteen years. These animals not only shunned anything found dead, but they were silent, never advertising their presence with the vocal serenades so much a part of normal coyote behaviour. In Jim Camp's opinion, "Sure as hell they've got nothing to cheer, so they've quit cheering."

Misty's mother and father had been among the few who learned that only live things were safe to eat, and they had taught her well, although she and two others were the only ones left of three litters born of her mother, before she fell one morning to the bullet of a rifleman who shot her just to see her fall.

84

Her father, Big Grey, was an unusually large coyote and also the sire of her pups; a very rare relationship developed in a completely abnormal environment where all coyotes, and other things as well, walked in the shadow of a horrible death.

Human thoughtlessness and ingenuity had laid the groundwork for the breeding of a super animal with a higher level of intelligence than previous generations had known. Line-breeding, wherein a father serves a daughter, can ruin a species by accentuating weaknesses. In this instance, however, there were no weaknesses; the pendulum had swung far the other way, and so a greater strength of intelligence, muscle and bone was being built up and welded into something stronger and more efficient than had ever existed before.

Livestock breeders have known of line-breeding for a long time. The ancient Arab horse became the wonderful, hardy and swift breed known for its beauty and intelligence that it is today, thanks to line-breeding. The various breeds of cattle and horses were established by line-breeding unusual and distinctive bulls and stallions to their own progeny. Virtually every kind of domesticated animal has been developed into different breeds in the same fashion. Now the sheepmen were blindly defeating their own purpose by inadvertently promoting a wondrous breed of coyote, superlative in its intelligence.

Big Grey was such a coyote. He was not only big and smart but very destructive, a habitual sheep killer ranging far and wide, mostly under cover of night. No herd left overnight out of a tight pen or shed was safe from him. When he killed an animal, he fed on it and never returned. When he got hungry, he killed again, sometimes miles away. He killed over such a wide stretch of country that it seemed to the suffering sheepmen that they were being victimized by many coyotes. If anyone had suggested that only one coyote

86

was trimming their herds, they would have scoffed. Big Grey managed to keep them in a continuous ferment, which in one case was helped out by the sheep owner's own dog.

This man was likely the most active advocate of poison in the country; a man who had to have his hate pointed somewhere and coyotes had become his target. When sheep began to be killed in his yard within a short distance of his house; his rage was near apoplexy.

Late one night he heard a disturbance among the sheep bedded down close to his buildings, and immediately he and his son jumped into the ranch pick-up with a loaded shotgun between them. They had barely left the yard, when the lights of the truck revealed a lamb lying dead and bloody at the edge of a patch of weeds. Beyond it, partially hidden by tall thistles, there was a movement and a glimpse of fur. The sheepman slid out of the cab, the shotgun coming to his shoulder, and a second later it belched shot and fire. The man knew a surge of elation as he saw the animal in the weeds go down in a heap, but when he found his own dog lying dead with wool in its teeth and blood on its muzzle, he was utterly deflated. He swore his son to secrecy and went right on hating coyotes, but when the boy's mother enquired about the missing dog her son told her what had happened. She confided in a friend who in turn confided in another, and the story was out.

In the meantime, Big Grey went right on killing.

Misty had never killed a sheep, nor did she feed on dead ones or allow her pups to do so. She was a small game specialist, an eater of mice, ground squirrels, hares and the occasional bird. Sometimes, when they were thick and ripe, she ate berries, like all coyotes. Earlier that year, when the pups began to hunt with her, she had shown them how to catch and eat grasshoppers. Together, they spent hours filling up on these insects, abundant along a little creek not far from the den.

This frosty morning, they were after mice. Following her lead, the four pups fanned out across the meadow, walking slowly, pausing here and there to listen, then suddenly pouncing to pin a mouse under their front feet. The little rodent would be picked up by the probing canine teeth, chewed and swallowed with a certain relish. The hunting was excellent, but none of the coyote family were so preoccupied as to be unwary. They often stood stock still for a moment looking and listening for any kind of intrusion. There was always at least one nose and one set of eyes and ears out of the five busy searching for danger. Misty was particularly watchful, regularly lifting her head to point her nose in various directions. Her eyes combed the skyline on both sides of the draw, but she did not see the cab of a truck parked in a slight hollow on a little-used farm road crossing the head of the draw, a few hundred yards away.

Inside it, Henry Tanner, a county councillor, sat with his near window rolled down and his eye glued to a powerful spotting scope trained on the coyotes.

Three days before, he had found one of his pure-bred ewes with its throat torn out, its liver and a portion of haunch eaten. Ordinarily his predator losses were light, for he was a careful man who penned his sheep at night, but this ewe had somehow been missed, and although he had no way of knowing this, Big Grey had found her at dawn. Next day a poisoned bait had been put out on the councillor's land.

There was nothing new in this; such bait had been on his land for years. *Station No. 6* it was called on the county map kept at the main office, and it had had some effect, but when the councillor reflected on his losses from predators, he wondered why they had increased slightly over the past two years. If the poison was working as expected, why was he able to see five coyotes such a short distance from it? Although he and Jim Camp did not see eye to eye in all things, he had a grudging respect for this man who loved wild things and spent so much time working to preserve them. Maybe there was something to his idea that the poison was no longer working the way it used to.

Even though Henry Tanner was only in municipal politics, he was as sensitive to criticism as any federal politician, and lately that criticism had been growing. He was observant enough to know that it might be a single coyote that was killing sheep in his section of the county and he wondered if it was one of the five he was now watching. He was also stubborn, and like most of his fellow councillors, he was not inclined to oppose a policy of such long standing as the poison campaign. Most of the farmers and cattlemen were ambivalent about the use of 1080; it was the scattering of sheepmen who were the pressure group. He also knew that many sheepmen were careless in their methods of looking after their stock.

From where he sat watching the coyotes, he could also see the bait to the south of them; a sixty-pound chunk of horse meat on top of a knoll, fastened to the ground with steel pins.

When they had been mousing just over half an hour, Misty led the way up the slope, the wind in her face and the pups strung out in a line behind her. At the rim of the draw, they paused to look and listen before setting out at a trot toward a range of low hills to the south. This route took them down wind from the bait, and when they were still some distance from it, their noses caught its smell. Misty stopped, the pups attentive around her as their keen noses absorbed the scent of raw meat.

It was exciting to them, but not to their mother, for she had known this spot all her life. Her mother had brought her to it two years before as part of her training as a pup.

Again she broke into a trot, this time leading the way through the long grass directly to the bait. She led the pups right up to it, stopping only a few yards away and assuming a rigid stance, the hair of her ruff and shoulders slowly rising straight up. The pups gathered around her, apprehensive because her attitude spoke of threatening danger, but nonetheless excited at the prospect of a feed of meat.

Misty remained frozen until one of her litter started nervously toward the meat, then she gave a sharp alarm bark, and rushed the pup to slash wickedly at its shoulder with her teeth, driving it back. She then resumed her attitude of alertness until another pup tried to go to the tempting lure; she punished this one too and drove it back. Any notion that she might be promoting a game was quickly dispelled by her sharp teeth. Each of the pups tried to go past her several times, but her reaction was an adamant refusal to allow it. A female, the smallest of the litter, tried to make a circle and come in from the far side, but was treated so roughly that she retired to the rear and crouched on her belly in the grass, showing no more interest.

Henry Tanner muttered softly to himself as he watched the mother coyote training her young to keep away from the bait. If he told the story of this morning's observations to his fellow councillors, they would likely not believe it. However, its meaning was unmistakable; coyotes were learning about the deadly 1080 poison. He was preoccupied as he watched the coyotes disappear over the skyline and headed his vehicle for home.

Over the days ahead, Misty continued to bring her pups back to the bait to teach them of its deadly danger. She kept it up until the three males no longer showed the slightest interest. The small female never tried to approach it after the first lesson; she just flattened out to wait for the routine to end.

As the winter continued with intermittent snow storms blowing out of the north, Misty's pups left her to scatter in search of food. Sometimes they met and briefly fraternized, no longer as a family, but simply following the social habits

90

of their kind. Occasionally they passed the bait while travelling through that portion of the country, but they always ignored it.

One dark night, the little female came near the bait on the downwind side. The bitter northeast breeze had brought snow and it was twenty below zero. She was ravenously hungry, and when the smell of meat hit her nose she went closer. Step by step she came, her muscles on a hair-trigger of caution, tight as a fiddle string, as though she expected the horse meat to jump at her. Finally she came to a stop with her nose right over it. Nothing happened. Only the wind moaned and the flying snow hissed around her. There was no foreign smell, only the seductively beckoning odour of meat.

Tentatively she began scraping away at the iron-hard meat with her nipping teeth, loosening fibres of it and swallowing them hungrily. It took a long time to get even a good mouthful or two off it, and soon she began to feel the first small, uneasy pangs of sickness urging her to turn away and begin travelling again. As she went, the sick feeling became worse, and several times she stopped to retch, but aside from a little yellowish stomach fluid nothing came up, for the small quantity of meat she had swallowed had moved quickly into her intestines.

Two hours later, she lay down in a clump of brush in the bottom of a draw, her lips drawn back from her teeth in a tortured grimace, squirming from the terrible pain cutting inside her like small, sharp blades. She stood up and lay down, and retched repeatedly. It gave her no relief but she kept it up till her eyes turned glassy, with a wild, mad look, seeing little and recognizing even less. There were only the waves of tearing, fiery pain that ripped and tore inside her.

Then, half-blindly, she began to run, paying no attention to her direction, the contours of the hills or anything in her path, but running with a queer, staggering gait like a mechanical thing, in a nightmare of never-ending torture. She ran into a patch of wild roses growing thickly on the lee side of a hill, where she rolled over several times in scrambling falls, her teeth chattering steadily as she whimpered and bit at herself and everything around her. She suddenly broke out of the bushes at a ninety-degree angle to her former course, to stagger down a long slope toward a brilliant farm-yard light on a high post.

Maybe the light attracted her through the haze of her pain. Maybe she never saw it. She came into the hard, bluish circle of its illumination in a twisting, limping run that took her under a truck parked near the yard's perimeter. Her head banged hard against ungiving steel and she went down, screwing herself into a squirming ball with her head finally appearing underneath her flank in a corkscrewing contortion. She rolled in shuddering convulsions, accompanied by the steady chattering of her teeth. She came to her feet heading into the brilliance reflected from hard-packed snow. Colliding with a truck tire, she bit at it before scrambling clear and continuing across the yard, where she ran head-on into the side of the barn. Bouncing off the concrete, she hit it again at an angle. Leaning against the wall, she slid along, her churning feet propelling her toward the crack of a slightly open door. Her nose went into the opening and the door gave a little more to allow her entry. Inside she staggered along the track of light from the crack until she banged her head on the side of a horizontally slatted box stall. Without pausing, she scrambled straight up, her feet flailing for a toehold between the planks. Over the top she went, to fall squarely on the back of one of two yearling bulls bedded on the other side.

The bulls jumped up in a panic, milling and snorting as this strange thing squirmed under their feet, the smell of it fetid in their noses and their ears assailed by the weird, unbroken chattering of its teeth. They bucked and plunged, wild-eyed as they tried to climb out over the walls of the stall but these were too high and stout to allow escape. Their hooves stomped and churned the straw of their bedding until there was no movement under them any more; only the smell remained, mixed with the odour of blood. The body of the coyote was a pulpy rag — delivered from the torture that had driven her for six long miles.

When the farmer came to the barn in the morning, he found his prize purebred bulls standing, still wild-eyed, clouds of steam rising from their backs. Discovery of the carcass under their feet filled him with apprehension. How could a coyote get into the box stall? It had to be crazy! The erratic tracks in the snow told a story that made no sense. Poison never occurred to him. Rabies came to his mind and his heart sank, for these were ribbon-winning bulls — the best he had ever raised. With a long face he went to the phone and called the veterinarian.

The vet came quickly and examined the bulls. Apart from a raw scratch or two on their feet and legs made by contact with the edges of the planks walling them in, they were uninjured. There was no way for him to be sure how the scratches had been made, but if the coyote had caused them and if she did have rabies, the bulls were doomed. He suspected poison as he examined the remains, but apart from its head the carcass was a bloody pulp. Analysis of heart and liver tissue in a specially equipped laboratory was the only way the tiny traces of 1080 could be identified, but there was no such tissue left. Swearing with great feeling, he cut off the coyote's head. At least they could detect rabies from the brain tissue if it wasn't too badly mangled.

When the lab report came back a few days later, it told him what he expected to hear; there was no rabies involved. For a while he was busy on the phone, and one of the calls was to his friend, the naturalist.

It was late February, the early part of the mating season for coyotes, when Misty and Big Grey began running together again. They met one night, when Big Grey was coming back from an unsuccessful sheep hunt on Henry Tanner's farm. After a preliminary sniffing of noses, Big Grey crowded close, examining Misty with care. The smell of her excited him even though she was not in heat yet. They romped briefly, making low chirping noises in their throats, then the dog coyote left off the play and went to a cinquefoil bush to urinate on it. He turned his back and made vigorous scratching motions with his hind feet, throwing up little clouds of snow that shone in the moonlight.

Again the two touched noses, and as though some unspoken message had been passed, they set off at a trot, the dog taking the lead. A mile to the south, he led the way into a draw and there they hunted abreast through some patches of saskatoon and chokecherry brush. The place was heavily tracked by jack rabbits, the big, prairie-roving varying hares that were passing back and forth from feeding among the threshed swaths of a field on the flats above. They suddenly jumped one and he shot away down the draw at a fast run, both coyotes in hot pursuit. For the first hundred yards, the hare interspersed his running with upward jumps propelled by his hind feet alone, as he looked back at his pursuers. They were closing fast, so he steadied into a flat-out run that left small puffs of snow standing behind him as he streaked up along the flanking slope of the draw.

Big Grey was fast and lost no distance behind the fleeing jack as it led the way in a long circular swing going behind a low butte. Misty slowed down to an easy gallop as she watched them go. Then she broke off at a sharp angle heading up onto the opposite side of the butte and flattened out behind a tuft of grass to watch. She did not have long to wait, for suddenly the jack came into view running hard with her mate driving it in her direction.

94

Misty remained motionless till the fleeing animal was almost even with her across the slope, before streaking out of her cover to cut it off, but her quarry dodged up the slope to cross behind her. She skidded into a sharp turn to come in behind it at a flashing run. Now it was Big Grey's turn to slack off his speed, as his mate pursued the hare at a long slant back down into the draw and up the other side.

Jack rabbits don't run in straight lines, and as Misty pressed this one hard, he began to bend inward again, his tracks scribbling a line that began to complete the final loop of a giant figure 8. As the rabbit shot downhill once more, Big Grey was loping easily towards the spot where its trail would cross itself to complete the figure. Without seeming to speed up for more than a couple of jumps, he intercepted the animal in a sudden flurry of snow punctuated by a wild, gurgling scream as his teeth closed on it. When Misty arrived a moment later, the hare hung limp in his jaws.

They shared the kill among frost crystals that glinted in the bright moonlight like diamond dust on the snow, taking the hare apart with dispatch and eating hungrily.

Over the next few days Big Grey attended Misty closely for she was coming into estrus. At the peak of it, he mated with her several times, and even though there was no competition, he never left her for a moment over a period of two days.

The third morning, they were hunting mice in a field a mile east of Henry Tanner's farm, when the smell of sheep came to their noses on the breeze. Misty paid it no attention, but Big Grey stood rooted in his tracks savouring the smell. It told him that sheep were on the move going out to pasture for the day. There's no way of telling what prompted him to give up his long-standing habit of hunting sheep only under cover of darkness, but he broke into a cross-country trot to investigate. Misty let him go alone.

The male's trail took him directly up wind through

hollows and slight folds of the country, and nowhere was he more than briefly skylined. He very artfully made use of the natural contours of the land, and when he came to the edge of the stubble field where the sheep were busily grazing, he crouched to watch them from a screen of grass and weeds along a fenceline there.

For a long time he remained flattened out absolutely motionless, his yellow eyes glinting as he watched.

A quarter mile beyond the flock and to one side, there was a low swell of ground partially hiding the farm buildings, with the tops of a row of trees showing beyond them. The slam of a door and the sound of a truck motor starting came to his ears, and then he heard the vehicle moving away. These were familiar sounds, for his ears had picked them up many times; he knew that they were linked with the movement of men and merely noted and kept track of them as he watched the sheep. As the sound of the motor faded, he came out of his hide at a long lope that took him directly to the herd.

Half a mile away, Henry Tanner drove his truck over a Texas gate to turn up a gravel road, heading for town. Out of long habit his eyes were roving towards his sheep when he saw them suddenly bunch and run. Slamming on the brakes, he reached into the glove compartment for his binoculars and a moment later he had the sheep in focus. He saw a coyote cut out a big ewe, run up alongside her, grab a throat hold and haul her down. Swearing with an angry passion, he dropped the glasses and gunned the truck into a quick turn, barely missing the ditch. He drove fast back to his house, where he ran inside to pick a rifle off its pegs and stuff some ammunition into its magazine. A minute or two later the truck was streaking for the field. Big Grey had swallowed no more than a few mouthfuls of hot meat, when he saw the truck come up on the swell of ground two hundred yards away.

As it came to a stop he headed out at a run. At the truck, the rifle barrel came out of the open window on the driver's side and steadied. The councillor was cool as he caught the fleeing coyote in the telescope sight. It was running broadside, a small target moving fast, but he knew how to shoot. Sweeping the sight's cross-hair from behind the target ahead of its nose, he squeezed the trigger without stopping the swing. Instantly, the coyote went down in a cloud of flying snow and rolled clear over. He could see it bite at itself as he chambered a fresh cartridge, and then it came to its feet heading for the fence at a plunging gallop. Again the man shot, the flat cracking report of the rifle echoing as the bullet kicked up dirt and snow a shade too high. The fleeing coyote went under the fence out of sight in a hollow beyond. An instant later the truck motor roared, its wheels spinning for traction as it headed toward a gate leading into the field beyond the fence.

Big Grey was running gamely in spite of a right front leg shot off half-way between elbow and ankle. Only a strip of skin still held it, flapping as he ran. He was bleeding badly, but he paid the wound no heed as he made a desperate effort to put distance behind him. Then, ahead of him on the skyline a quarter-mile away, the gleam of sun on metal caught his eye as the truck loomed up. Without slowing, he swerved away over a rise of ground into another hollow, where he doubled back toward the fence. Upon reaching it, he headed along it, behind the strip of growth left uncut between the fields, toward the head of a brushy draw half a mile away. He might have made it except for the crimson blood trail on the snow behind him.

It was so plain to Henry Tanner's eye that he didn't have to slow down to read its message; he simply swung the truck in a wide circle to cut the coyote off. He was waiting within easy range of the lip of the draw, when Big Grey arrived at a shambling run, his mouth open and his tongue lolling in his dash for cover. Again the rifle barrel came down, steadied and bucked as the bullet went on its way. Big Grey never heard the shot, dying instantly in mid-jump as the bullet took him through both shoulders.

Misty heard the shooting as she lay flattened out in low brush waiting for her mate. When no other sounds came, she curled up in a ball with her nose buried in her brush and slept. Several times during the day, she roused to look and listen, but it was dark when she trotted out into the wind along the tracks Big Grey had left that morning. She held her course — a grey moving shadow almost invisible in the gloom — until she came to the bloody trail left by her wounded mate. The hair lifted on her back and she stood very still for a while, looking and sniffing. Then she broke into a lope on a wide circle that took her back to the blood trail near the spot where Big Grey had made his last jump. She examined the place, her attitude one of hair-trigger alertness as she smelled blood, man and death.

Giving a low whimpering cry, she headed out in another big circle around the farmstead before bending back toward where she had spent the day. There she stopped on top of a knoll, completely motionless, as though communing with the stars. As if deciding something, she set out at a trot towards the southeast at a steady mile-eating gait, taking her well past the poison station.

The moon that hung overhead, lighting the country, was waning when she came to a big pasture on a ranch beyond the grain farms. In the long grass by a wide frozen slough, she began mousing, but stopped to listen to the distant sound of an engine coming from somewhere beyond a low ridge behind her. The sound grew stronger, and something broke into view on the skyline; a squat thing with lights that blazed, dipped and swung as the power toboggan came down the slope toward the slough. Standing motionless in the tall grass, Misty was invisible and she knew it. But the light beams sweeping back and forth over her were too much; she broke and ran out over the snow-covered ice.

Instantly, the young man on the toboggan saw her and swung the machine after her, letting out a long yell that was echoed by a squeal of excitement from the girl riding behind him. He had had supper at her home and was giving her a ride on his new machine, when they spotted the coyote.

Misty was caught in the powerful beams of the lights, and the motor was howling in her ears as she ran straight across the expanse of ice. She was heading for a fringe of willows on the far side, but the machine quickly overtook her, forcing her to dodge. The toboggan turned wide before straightening out behind her again. The girl, unaccustomed to riding high-speed turns, had allowed her weight to shift too far to the outside and was almost thrown off, and she yelped with fright as she clutched wildly at the driver's middle. This only added to the excitement, and he pushed the throttle wide open as he drove the toboggan hard after the fleeing coyote, bent on running her down. Again she was heading for the broken ground beside the lake, running in a tunnel of bright light, and again the roaring monster overtook her, forcing her to dodge. The whole procedure was duplicated.

Misty was tiring. Her mouth was wide open, her tongue hanging out the side, as she made a desperate bid to reach shore. The lights had her pinned but she was paying them less attention now, and dodged out of them. The driver, anticipating her move, jockeyed his throttle into an easier turn, spotlighting her, and again pressing hard.

The howling nightmare was right on her heels; Misty cut sharply to the side, but slipped and somersaulted over onto her back and the toboggan shot past. Before the boy could bring it around, she was up again to put her last energy into a streaking run for a point of grass sticking out onto the snow-covered ice.

The front runners were six feet from her tail when she reached the grass, the driver seeing only the coyote as his machine hit the snow-draped growth. The next instant both runners hit the frozen side of a muskrat house with a smashing bump, throwing the machine high into the air. Both riders left it, falling to one side like rag dolls, and it landed upside-down with a crash.

Misty was again running alone, the horrifying noise behind her suddenly silent.

Back at the toboggan, nothing moved. After some minutes the young man stirred where he lay in the snow, and groaned as the ends of the broken bones in his arm ground into his flesh. A few feet away from him, low whimpering sobs came from the girl, only half-conscious, blood streaming from a deep gash in her cheek. For them it was going to be a long way home.

On a hilltop half a mile away, Misty stood gasping for breath, her sides heaving as she looked back. There was no sign of the thing that had come so close to catching her, and she scooped up a mouthful of snow to cool herself before setting out again at a slow lope. When the rising sun painted the snowy hills along the Waterton River pale pink, she found a nest of dry leaves under a fallen log in the midst of a grove of giant cottonwoods, and curled up to sleep. Her life had been the prize in her great race, and she had won it. Never again did she return to her old range.

Poison Station No. 6's record that winter accounted for just one coyote, two rare feruginous rough-legged hawks, two badgers, five skunks and sundry small animals. All either ate the bait, or fed on the bodies of its victims.

Out at the north end of the county a similar bait set on a small sheep farm had a much more impressive count. This location was close to a forest reserve where poison was not allowed, consequently a normal coyote population

100

habitually ranged through the surrounding ranchlands. Apart from a heavy toll of coyotes, however, one bald eagle, three golden eagles and other birds and animals, including John Severn's highly trained stock dog, were destroyed.

Severn owned a cattle ranch between the bait and the forest reserve. He had no use for poison and had complained about it with no more success than Jim Camp. When his dog came staggering home, he immediately knew what had happened, and rushed it to the veterinary clinic, but it was dead by the time he got there. Leaving the dead dog at the clinic, he drove his pick-up along Main Street into the middle of town.

This late March morning was warm and balmy with the smell of spring in the air. The cottonwood buds were swelling and the ground was muddy from the thawing of winter's snow and frost. Jim Camp stood in front of the general store on the sunny side of the street enjoying the warmth. His wide-brimmed hat was pulled low, and under it, out of long habit, his eyes constantly roamed, missing no activity along the busy street. He saw John Severn's truck pull into a space along the curb half a block away, the door open and the tall familiar figure of the rancher step out and walk to the sidewalk, where he stood looking both ways. Severn spotted the naturalist and came toward him. It was immediately evident that something was very wrong.

"Hello, John," Jim greeted him, "You look mad as an old he-couger with his tail caught between a rock and a hard place! Something bothering you?"

"Sure as hell!" came the rejoinder, and John Severn told what had happened to his dog. "And that ain't all by a damn sight!" he gritted between his teeth. "That bait is barely a mile from my door. About two weeks ago a poisoned coyote came staggerin' into the yard on his last legs, his mouth slobberin' and his teeth chatterin'. He was humpin' along, gettin' up and fallin' down blind as a bat, and he went under

101

my car right by the door and rolled around bangin' his head on the bottom of it. I took my .22 rifle and got down flat to shoot him. He was movin' around and I couldn't see very good, so I missed the first time and blew a hole in a tire. And if that ain't bad enough, a while before that, I found another one floatin' around dead in the water trough at the big spring back of the buildings. I've been to see the council several times and all I get is the run-around. Ain't these people got an ounce of sense?"

"What did you do with the carcasses?" Jim asked.

"Buried 'em under some loose rock, but I might as well have just let 'em lay! I got dead coyotes all over the ranch. They come down off the forest reserve to get at the bait, get a bellyful of poison and then head back. The warm weather bein' earlier than usual this year thawed the meat, and they can eat a hundred times more than it would take to kill 'em. They don't last long, and sure as hell, there's a lot of poison on my ranch I don't want there!"

For a few moments Jim Camp was silent, then he said, "I have the provincial act here and it says the county can't put poison on privately owned land without permission. I'm on my way to check it for sure at the lawyer's office."

The rancher grunted. "You know it'll take forever to convince the council. I want somethin' done now!"

Again the naturalist was quiet, but then he showed his teeth in a mischievous grin. "By rights those dead coyotes on your land belong to the county. Why don't you gather them up and deliver them to their office door right here in town? They own them, and maybe that would give them something to think about."

John Severn's face softened a bit in a smile as he said, "Sure as hell those coyotes are high enough in this weather to make a good impression. They have their regular meeting next Monday. About when they come back from lunch would be a good time I think. Will you come with me?"

102

"Sure thing," Jim promised. I'll meet you at the east end of town shortly after noon. In the meantime, there might be something I can think of that will help a bit." Then he added, "The town may not like this much. We could find ourselves in trouble up to our ears."

The rancher grunted. "Too bad! If you're game, I'll take the chance." Then he grinned. He was already savouring the satisfaction of dumping a bunch of rotting coyotes on the immaculate lawn by the front door of the county building.

As he drove toward home, the naturalist was thinking that it was a strange thing when two ordinarily law-abiding citizens took off on a caper like this. If it came to trouble, they could cross that bridge when they got to it. The laugh wrinkles around his eyes deepened and he whistled a merry little tune.

When he got home, he made a few phone calls before his wife called him for lunch. She looked at him contemplatively as he sat down at the table and remarked, "You look like you've had a good morning. As a matter of fact you look so downright tickled about something, you can hardly stand it. How come?"

She listened, wide-eyed with astonishment, as he told her what he and John Severn planned to do, but she hated the poison as much as he did and knew it would do no good to try to talk him out of it anyway. "You'll both likely land in jail!" she exclaimed. "Edith and I will come visit once in a while." More soberly, she asked, "What do you think will happen?"

"We'll just have to wait and see," her husband said, and applied himself to a full plate of stew with gusto.

Shortly after noon on Monday, Jim Camp drove into town from the south just in time to see John Severn's truck coming in from the north. They both pulled into a vacant lot near Main Street, and got out. The back of Severn's pick-up had its load concealed by a big plastic tarp.

Jim walked around to the down-wind side of it and came to a sudden stop, exclaiming, "Holy smoke! That's enough to knock down a skunk! How many have you got in there?"

"Ten of 'em!" John replied, folding back a corner of the tarp with a flourish to reveal a mass of coyote carcasses, all in a state of extreme disrepair — some had been picked open by birds; every one was smelling to heaven in the warm sun.

"Keep them covered," the naturalist advised. "We don't want to attract attention yet."

At that moment two cars pulled up beside them; vehicles carrying the names of a city TV station and a newspaper. John looked a bit startled, but Jim grinned and introduced him to the two men who got out of the cars, "Meet a couple of friends, John. I thought it would be a good idea to get some publicity for the festivities. I hope you don't mind. After all, the tender spot on the belly of the bull that we're locking horns with *is* publicity."

John Severn's grin widened as he shook hands, and he said, "It's about time. Let's go!"

Five minutes later, the truck backed up to the curb in front of the county building. When the newsmen had readied their cameras and lined them up, the naturalist and the rancher slid the load out of the pick-up and arranged it carefully on the green lawn to one side of the walk near the foot of the steps. The big TV camera on its tripod kept interested passers-by on the move. Those coming from the west looked curious till they got past, then they hurried to get out of range of the awful smell. Those coming the other way looked as though they couldn't believe it, and hurried by upon reaching sweet air. The sight of the camera put a damper on any comments that might have been made, for most people are shy about being filmed. Only one, a portly gentleman on his way to his office after lunch, stared hard and growled, "What the hell. . . !" then, seeing the camera, changed his mind and hurried away.

104

Finally the councillors came from their lunch, heading back to their meeting chamber. They came down wind so had no warning of events to come till they were confronted by the pile of coyotes. They came singly or in groups of two or three, so their reactions were separate, but all were identical. They stared in utter disbelief, stopped, rooted in their tracks, looking as though they were about to explode, then they saw the camera. The sight of it unnerved them completely, for a TV camera means just one thing to politicians — a public appearance with the possibility of their words as well as their pictures being broadcast. This surprise, catching them without preparation, shut them up as effectively as a gag. Only the reeve enquired, with severe and obvious disapproval, "What's this all about?"

Jim Camp answered him with quiet firmness. "Gentlemen, these are your coyotes. They were scattered all over John Severn's ranch, and he doesn't want them there. We thought we should bring them to you."

In an unusual but understandable phenomenon of human nature, none of the collected councillors gave any orders. Had just one given firm directions about where to take the carcasses, they would have been followed, but they filed up the steps and disappeared inside the building without saying another word. This took the conspirators completely by surprise, so they waited, but after considerable time had passed, they became justifiably restless.

"Well I'll be damned," muttered the rancher. "Ain't somebody going to move?"

"I've got lots of pictures but very little dialogue," commented the television cameraman. Looking at his watch, he added, "I'd like to stay, but time is crowding me. It should make a great story anyway."

"Let's all go," the naturalist suggested. "They'll appreciate 'em more, if they have to arrange the burial by themselves."

So they left the coyotes there, simmering in the hot sun. Behind them, the councillors were forted up in their chamber, and the place was in an uproar. Never had the council faced anything like this. Some councillors were seething with anger, and a motion to lay a charge was duly made and seconded. "What charge, gentlemen?" the chairman asked. "We'd better be very sure."

Nobody could agree, so the act was brought out and studied, but that only compounded the argument.

Meanwhile Henry Tanner had been quietly studying a copy of the provincial act, and now he broke into the discussion, "Mr. Chairman, I've been looking at the law governing pesticides. I'm sorry to say I've never really looked closely at it before. We all know we've had complaints. I really don't blame John Severn, because he's had trouble and he's entitled to be mad as a hornet. Let's face it, we've been using poison more as a habit than anything else. But when it comes to the law, I think we may be as guilty as hell ourselves." He paused to let this sink in and then suggested, "I move that we adjourn and take some time for further study of this matter."

When the story broke on television and radio and in the newspapers next day, it did nothing to sweeten tempers. Although Henry Tanner was angry, he could not help a sly grin. When John Severn and Jim Camp chose to kick the lid off the pot, they kicked it high, wide and handsome. Although he had no use for their methods, he admired their guts and couldn't altogether condemn them.

So the controversy boiled and simmered. There were meetings and more arguments, while the instigators of the insurrection listened and waited. When the whole thing began to cool down, one thing was certain: in that county poison would never again be used without thought of its possible political consequences.

Meanwhile, oblivious to it all, a mother coyote tended

her pups in a den near the head of the creek that ran through Jim Camp's ranch.

Misty's new home was located in idyllic surroundings on a gravelly slope overlooking a swamp. Aspen and willow groves separated the meadows that stretched away on both sides of her den site. Directly in front of the den, the swamp lay, greening-up now with patches of cattails and slough grass. To the south and west the Rockies stood, snow-capped and rugged, wild as they had been when man first saw them.

Misty was lean from continual hunting, and her dugs sagged from the demands of six hungry pups. Her days were spent stalking and killing the fat ground squirrels that scampered abundantly over the meadows.

One morning Jim Camp, screened by new green leaves, watched through his binoculars as a squirrel sunned itself on the dirt mound in front of its den. A hundred yards from the squirrel, Misty lay flattened out behind a little cinquefoil bush, watching it fixedly. She was as motionless as a bronze image. Finally, the squirrel roused itself and began to feed on the lush green grass, moving toward her. Not a whisker moved on the mother coyote until the small animal was well away from its hole. Suddenly she shot from cover, streaking half-way toward it before it saw her. The squirrel fled with chirping cries of alarm, but it was too late, for the coyote's jaws snapped shut on it and she shook her head, killing the animal instantly. Then she trotted back to her den.

The naturalist watched her go with a smile deepening the sun-browned lines of his face. "Cheers, old lady," he murmured softly. "Things are coming together again."

Billy's Dangerous Game

We came into the upper valley by packtrain, our string of loaded horses picking their way along the trail at an easy walk, the way mountain packhorses do in rough country near the end of the day — tired but content in knowing they will soon be unloaded. Near timberline on a lush meadow close to a cheerful, ice-cold, sparkling little stream, I stepped down from my lead horse, and before long we were surrounded by organized confusion with packs and saddles scattered everywhere on the grass. Soon the tents were up, and in an hour everything was snug: smoke drifting from the chimney that protruded from the cooktent roof, as the cook busied herself with preparations for supper; the wranglers covering the stacked saddles against weather and the possible visit of a salt-hungry porcupine; and our guests wandering about in the warm late-afternoon sun enjoying the view. As always I was reminded of how little it takes to make people happy in wilderness country; some canvas to keep out the weather, plenty of dry firewood, sufficient good food, a dry, warm sleeping robe; all amid surroundings that are the playground of the gods.

Taking my binoculars, I walked out to the far edge of the meadow to examine the cliffs of the Continental Divide towering over our camp. The great wall of rock stretched for a couple of miles, serrated, rugged, and in some places absolutely sheer to a skyline some two thousand feet above. The talus fans below were criss-crossed with bighorn and mountain goat trails. Half a mile to the south my glasses picked up six big rams with heavy curling horns, feeding at the base of the cliffs. Then, half way up, on a jutting shoulder to my right, a big white mountain goat appeared, to stand in rugged silhouette against the blue sky. He was joined by two more. All were billies, and all were curiously staring at the feeding horses and the white tents.

Goats can be phlegmatic creatures at times, showing little fear of man when they feel secure on some height where the topography reaches for the vertical, sometimes even surpasses it, and affords a great choice of escape terrain. Slab-sided and narrow through the body, with short, sharp horns, they are designed by nature to walk cliff ledges so narrow that no other animal, except the occasional hungry cougar and man, will even attempt them. The mountains are their fortresses, cannily used as a defense against all intruders.

They are primitive, though intelligent, animals living in a harsh austere country. Sometimes they'll spend days in a place where every step is either up, down or along a miniscule ledge, and a slip would spell a shattering fall. But stumbling is not part of a goat's make-up. Only once have I seen one in trouble, when a nubbin of rock broke off as the goat lifted his weight onto it. The billy turned in the air and came down on another tiny outcrop about ten feet below, in perfect balance. It did not even shake his composure, for very deliberately he turned and climbed back up where he had wanted to go.

From the time they are tiny kids no bigger than a

miniature poodle, mountain goats live on the craggy faces of the mountains in winter and in summer. It is mighty impressive to watch a nanny leading the way up a cliff, with no more concern than a human mother would display while wheeling her baby carriage along a city sidewalk, while behind the goat her youngster jumps and scrambles in an effort to keep up on its short legs and tiny feet. With seeming heartlessness, she rarely looks back to see how her young one is making out. It is as though she knows it must learn to keep up in order to live in such demanding surroundings. Sometimes a ledge that she climbs over with ease gives the kid trouble, so it must find a way around, and it falls behind. At times like this, it is vulnerable to a hunting eagle. If the youngster suffers an injury from a falling rock or has any kind of physical defect, it usually perishes. Though this seems cruel, it is nature's way of weeding out the weaklings. Only the strong survive in the mountains.

Mountain goats have always been something of a challenge and a fascination to me, both as a naturalist and as a wildlife photographer, and so I watched the three billies looking down at our camp with more than just a passing interest.

Moving my binoculars back and forth over the cliffs, I studied its details looking for possible routes up to their stronghold. Meanwhile, the billies moved about, striking poses tempting to one with a passion for photography. When I went to supper, they had disappeared into a steep chimney carved into the solid rock by the falling water of thousands of spring run-offs.

At sunrise next morning, they were back in plain view, lying comfortably on a promontory directly over our camp. After seeing our guests off for a day's fishing at a nearby lake, I put some lunch and my camera into a light rucksack, laced on my climbing boots and set off toward the cliff for a day with the goats.

I was much younger then and I firmly believed that a man who knew how to free-climb could follow goats anywhere they chose to go. Having grown up and lived the greater part of my life among the high crags of the Alberta and British Columbia Rockies, mountain terrain was a way of life for me, and I enjoyed the exhilaration and challenges that go with climbing.

Why do people climb mountains? A very famous climber once answered this question by saying, "Because they are there." But for me, the presence of the peaks is only part of it; the many kinds of life found on the rugged faces of the mountains makes them even more irresistably fascinating and breathtakingly beautiful.

The highlights of exploration and adventure balance the costs of sinew-stretching exertion, pounding heart and labouring lungs. The danger is tempered by physical fitness and the knowledge that one may be treading where no man has ever trod before. There are, to be sure, some moments when muscles fairly groan, and when concentration is an exhausting thing, but there are also experiences so utterly beautiful that they are imprinted on the mind forever.

Once, for example, I was crossing the foot of a sheer lava intrusion and I came to a tiny waterfall sparkling and splashing like a fountain into a perfect bowl carved out of the solid black lava. To one side of it there was a small grotto, where a bubble in the molten rock had broken. This was partially screened by the frothy, light green lace of maiden-hair ferns. Behind them I saw the glint of reflections from the falling water and when I moved closer to look, there was the sudden flash of wings as a bird flew out. I knelt to part the ferns and found the inside of the hole lined with quartz crystals glittering like jewels. Artfully built in this little cave was the nest of a Townsend's solitaire with four greenish-blue eggs. My camera was primitive and colour film was still in the future, so photographing it was

112

impossible, but the image still lives with me as one of the most exquisitely beautiful I have ever seen; a shrine in lovely homage to a mountain.

Then there was the time I sat on a broad ledge with my back to a rock wall just as morning was opening its sleepy eyes. I was overlooking a secret pass with ranks of massive peaks — miles and miles of them all purple and rose and gold in the sunrise.

I had spent every daylight hour on that ledge for seven long days hoping to film a big grizzly who lived in the area. My grub was running low back at camp, time was beginning to press, the rock was very hard under my hip pockets and my jacket was too light to keep out the chilly breeze playing capriciously among the mountain battlements around me. Patience is a virtue acquired by those who film wild things, especially grizzlies, but mine was wearing mighty thin.

Suddenly, out of some shintangle scrub below, the great bear appeared and all the discomfort and waiting was forgotten. Closer and closer he came, walking up the pass into the sunlight, his silvery coat glistening and rolling in cadence with his muscles, and his long front claws glowing dully like old ivory. There was a power and grace about him that is synonymous with grizzlies. He turned directly toward me to come up a steep snowdrift to a point right under my boot toes. For a moment, he stood still, a king of the mountains looking out over his wild realm, and then he sat down to slide in merry abandon to the bottom.

The motion picture camera whirred as it recorded the scene on film, catching him as he came back up to repeat the performance — royalty setting aside its dignity to enjoy a frolic. After such a long wait, it was tremendously exciting to catch this action in the lens of my camera. I did not know it then, but the light was being reflected from the snow as I was shooting into the sun, and my electronic meter was lying to me. The resulting pictures were an unusual record but useless for anything else. Just the same, the scene so indelibly printed in my mind is almost a tangible thing, something of great value to stay with me as long as I live.

That is why I climb mountains, enduring the storms and enjoying the sun. These and a thousand other experiences keep me climbing, and make me always wonder what will unfold over the next ridge or beyond the next bend of some wild canyon.

This day I had goats in mind. The solid footing of rock on the cliff face was welcome after the drudgery of climbing the loose rock of the talus fan where my mountain boots slid back a step for every two taken upward. My muscles were loose and I was feeling good as I worked out a route up to the goats' level, although their exact location was now hidden from me by a bulge of the mountain.

I did not hurry. Every handhold and foothold was carefully tested, and following an old rule of free-climbing, one hand and one foot were always well anchored for every move. There is a certain rhythm to this, a fluidity of motion. The climber makes the best use of every feature of the rock and distributes his weight as evenly as possible to enhance his balance. All moves are deliberate, and are made with confidence and purpose.

As each step of my route was worked out, I paused to carefully appraise the next. This served a double purpose, giving me a chance to rest and time to plan, for one does not backtrack if it can be avoided. To do so is like taking money out of a savings account; it takes time and more effort to replace it.

Finally I reached a wider ledge on the same level as the goats, about two-thirds of the way up the cliff, but they were still out of sight somewhere to the north of me. Travelling along the ledge, I climbed to the top of a jutting buttress just in time to see the shaggy rear of a billy disappear around a corner two hundred feet ahead. I followed, and this time was rewarded by a good view of the goats, as they stood in line at a spot where the ledge narrowed and pitched down at a slant around another corner. Two of them were watching me, obviously aware of my company up here in the airy hallways of their mountain fortress.

Ahead of them there was a sheer wall, impossible for anything but a fly, and I wondered what route they would choose to get past it. If they cut back above me, they would be forced to pass close, for there was another impassable cliff, overhung in places, above me. Their most likely route was a cutback below, so I stepped ahead into full view and approached them. They immediately moved ahead climbing down along the ledge around the curve at a walk.

Upon reaching the point where they had disappeared, I was astonished to see them all lined up on the tiny ledge where it faded out to nothing on the sheer wall. In paying more attention to what is behind than what is ahead, they had trapped themselves.

Now I cut off their retreat, and they all had their heads turned, looking back at me somewhat quizzically as though wondering what to do next, their hoofs splayed as they gripped the ledge, and their high, narrow bodies balanced perfectly, though mighty precariously, on the bare edge of nothing. I did not have long to wonder what they would do. Almost in unison, they reared and pivoted outward on their hind feet to land facing me, and then they came marching purposefully back as though saying that they were getting out of there, and it would be just too bad for me if I was in the way. Behind and above me there was a narrow, almost perpendicular, chimney that could be reached quickly if it became necessary, so I stayed to see what they would do.

On they came till the leader was only about ten short steps away. There he halted, and I detected definite anger. His ragged, half-shed mane stood up like a warlock as he bowed his neck, displaying his short, black, curved horns, sharp as needles, and he pawed the rock with a front foot. Then he began chewing — grinding his teeth ominously in what appeared to be a towering rage. Ready to retreat quickly into the chimney, I spoke to him softly and took a step in his direction. This obviously surprised all three billies, and again they swapped ends to head back down the ledge. Upon reaching the dead-end, they gave the cliff another hard look and once more made that spectacular turn to come back.

This time it was obvious that they meant business, and I quickly scrambled out of the way into the chimney, where I turned my back to the cliff face, braced my boots on each side of it and picked up a fist-sized stone to discourage an invasion. The goats passed me at a fast walk barely fifteen feet below, not one so much as glancing my way, and disappeared around the corner. Although there was a camera hanging on a strap around my neck, I could not use it, being too busy with more important things, like hanging on to the mountain.

When I climbed back down onto the ledge and made my way to the point, I found that the billies had taken a route that slanted down the mountain. As I watched, they switched to their original direction below me, pausing to give me a long stare before disappearing under an overhang. I followed and saw them reappear from under the overhang and pick their way casually along a ledge which led to a long vertical crack, or chimney, in the rock, several feet wide and directly under the face that had so effectively stopped them on their first try. Here centuries of spring run-offs had scoured the rock as smooth as the side of a bowl. The ledge they were following was cut off where it came out from under the overhang, and slanted upwards on the other side of the chimney. The gap was about six feet wide. The billies had no trouble passing the overhang, for it was high enough

116

to miss their backs. When they came to the gap in the ledge, they blithely jumped across and proceeded on up the other side. The awesome eagle thoroughfare below they ignored completely.

But I could not help being aware of it — not unduly afraid — just respectful. In climbing one becomes accustomed to heights and develops confidence through exposure. However, this place made me acutely aware of my limitations. It was time to pause and contemplate geography as well as the power of gravity.

The overhang posed a problem; while it had allowed the goats to pass, a six-foot man with a rucksack on his back would be cramped. The ledge was a foot wide in most places, flat and without any breaks till it reached the chimney; a mark for the positive, though no cause for a celebration. It sloped slightly downwards, leaving no room for mistakes.

It was not impossible, so I eased out step by step under the overhang. In places I could make headway by stooping low and planting my boots on the extreme outside edge of the ledge, but for the most part I was forced to face in to the rock and inch my way along using every available handhold. Friction was the only alternative to the pull of gravity. It was a kind of crab-wise routine in gymnastics where every handhold was tested, for the sedimentary rock was rotten and sometimes pieces of it came loose before I found a solid hold. The fragments fell in silence for a long way before clattering on projecting rocks below — not something to lull one into any kind of carelessness. It was a great relief to stand comfortably when I finally reached the chimney.

I wondered how any sensible person could ever get himself into a spot like this. The ledge ended here and the six-foot chasm had to be crossed, for backtracking held even less attraction. Not only was it a reversal of original intent, but I was far from sure that it could be done, because my route had taken me around a projecting rock which offered

117

little to hang onto in getting back. I had barred the door on myself — something that can be done in one step in such terrain — so across the gap it had to be, even though the prospect was hair-raising.

On a ledge ten feet above a green meadow such a manoeuvre would mean nothing, but here, with this abyss yawning at me, the prize offered for a slip was final.

As I stood studying the place, one of the billies came back to gaze down at me as though curious to find out what I would do now.

The problem in a spot like this is mostly psychological; the difficulty is exaggerated by the surroundings. The trick is to convince oneself of this fact. It's a matter of will and positive thinking, accompanied by the utter certainty that no mistake can be permitted. A hundred times that morning I had been in similar situations where a slip would have been just as deadly, though far less spectacular.

The goats had crossed. What they had done, I could do, I told myself; but they had four legs instead of two, four flexible, spongy hoofs to grip the rock and hold when they landed. If I could make the jump and come down in perfect balance, then crouch and grasp two handholds on the ledge ahead, I would be anchored. It was a contest between me and the mountain.

Stepping back far enough to let me take two quick steps, I took a big breath, and with every nerve concentrating on my landing, I leapt. My boots came down on solid rock. I leaned forward, flexing my knees to take the shock, and my fingers found their holds and dug in. For a long moment I did not move a fraction of an inch. Then came the sound of a little rock dislodged from the ledge as it clattered far below.

When I let out my breath and slowly stood up, my knees were trembling a bit and there was sweat pouring off me, even though the jump had been incredibly easy. I had moved on to the top of a buttress, before I became aware of sharp tingling pain on my right knee and elbow. A quick look revealed patches of skin scraped off, blood oozing from the raw spots where I had scraped against the rock wall over the ledge upon landing. The scrapes were sore, but it was a cheap enough exchange.

Ahead of me the goats were parading away in single file along a wide ledge leading to an easier portion of the cliff. They paused to stare back, and then moved away again, but I did not follow. Sitting with my back comfortably propped against a sloping rock, I ate my lunch and watched them go, content to let good enough alone. It occurred to me that they were probably the most dangerous animals in the mountains — not because of any threat from their sharp horns, but due to the kind of country they led their pursuers into among the peaks.

The lesson learned that morning stuck with me. Mountain goats can go where a lone climber has no business following, no matter how skilled that climber may be.

Now when I see a big, old billy posing like a statue atop a cliff against the blue sky and sailing clouds, I am inclined to tip my hat and say, "Happy days, old boy! It's your mountain and you're welcome to it!"

The Otters

From its headwaters in British Columbia, the Flathead River flows down into Montana, finally emptying into Flathead Lake. It is a wild and magnificent wilderness river at its upper end, lying couched between the high crags of the Rockies and a secondary range to the west. Both the river and its feeder lakes, hidden away among the flanking mountains, teem with fish, making it an otter heaven. It was in this wilderness paradise that Proo and Kim grew to adulthood.

Proo and Kim were river otters, young adults from families that lived and foraged along the North Fork of the Flathead River and its many tributaries. They mated in late winter, and the following summer they came up a creek flowing west out of Bowman Lake, to play and feed along its wild shores. Sleek, muscular animals of incredible grace, their movements were one long aquatic ballet as they pursued fish and played in the clear mountain waters.

They had Bowman Lake to themselves, for there were no other otters there, and what prompted them to move, there is no way to tell. But one September evening Kim led the way up another creek flowing out of a twisted canyon at the east end of the lake. They had explored this creek several times, but had always turned back at a bubble-strewn pool that lay at the foot of a high waterfall. This time, however, Kim led the way up the side of the canyon, along a series of ledges, through ferns and shrubbery to the top of the falls. There, they travelled steadily on up the stream toward its head, sometimes leaving it to detour around other falls, but generally staying with the water.

Almost as much at home on land as they are in water, the otters went at their flowing lope, so smooth it is deceptive in its speed, a gait that eats up the distance without seeming to be fast. Their route took them through heavy timber to timberline, where the larches were all gold in autumn dress, and where the creek flowed under overhanging canopies of alders and willows, rattling and rushing swiftly amongst boulders. At the first hint of dawn, the otters were on top of the pass straddling the Continental Divide, and here the creek was reduced to a trickle fed by remnants of melting snowdrifts that still lingered in the hollows.

They followed a well-marked trail until the black bulk of a big grizzly hove in sight over a rise in the paling light, prompting them to slip away to the side among some big, jagged rocks with the breeze in their favour. The travelling bear was unaware of them till he came to the musky scent of their tracks, when he paused, curiously sniffing, then disinterestedly continued on his way. The otters, meanwhile, had moved on over the crest of the pass to the head of another creek flowing northeast.

This was the headwaters of the Kootenai River, and Kim and Proo greeted the stream with enthusiastic splashing, though it was too small for anything but a swimming stroke or two in its deepest places. They looped through the shallows, slithered down steep little runs like wet silk ribbons, sometimes rolling in spiral twists, as fluid as the water in which they travelled. Side creeks fed the stream, and within a mile it was deep enough for swimming. They revelled in it, powerful sweeps of their muscular bodies shooting them through the pools like two big fish.

The stream was barren of fish, as nearly all high streams are, because trout are cut off from the headwaters by impassable falls in mountain country, so the fishing was bad, and the otters kept moving. They came to a water-worn chute, where the creek sluiced at a steep angle over smooth rock into a frothy pool effervescing with bubbles, and they shot happily down its length to arrive with scarcely a splash. Kim surfaced, snorting softly to clear his nose, and headed for shore, intending to climb back to the top and slide again.

He was still in the water, only his head showing on the surface, when his nose picked up a scent — a sweet, warm smell arresting his motion so that he drifted around behind a rock pointing like a weathervane into the current. Proo came alongside him and they both lifted their heads cautiously to look over a fringe of grass and other plants rimming a tiny meadow by the pool. Both otters sank and swam to the riffle downstream, coming to shore behind a screening clump of willows. Circling wide through a patch of alders, they came to the higher side of the little meadow, overlooking a covey of spruce grouse warming themselves and feeding in the first rays of the rising sun. The otters were among them before the birds were aware of their presence, and quick as light they pounced on two, killing them so fast there was scarcely a movement apart from the fluttering of wings as the survivors flew up into the small scrubby trees rimming the place.

When the otters had fed, there was nothing left but some feathers stirring a bit in the thermal breezes wafting up the slope. Proo and Kim touched noses briefly and then began rolling over and over, mouthing each other gently and wrestling in play, before stretching out in the sun among the greenery for a brief rest. They soon took to the water again, rolling and twisting around the pool in graceful undulations. Then, without any sign seeming to pass between the two, Kim suddenly pointed his nose downstream and shot away. Again they were travelling.

The creek rapidly grew into a small river, a fast mountain flow roaring and leaping over falls and down whitewater rapids, where the otters did not have to drive themselves but could drift with the stream. When they came to a falls that wasn't too high, they simply went over it in a long smooth dive; the higher ones were detoured in brief overland excursions through the dense forest that now crowded against the water. At one particularly high falls, a big driftwood log was standing on end, with the spray playing over its protruding snags of broken branches. The otters climbed down along its slippery, slanting trunk as though they had done it twenty times before, though it was completely new to them. Surefooted as cats and complete masters of their surroundings, they dove off it into the pool, hugging bottom till they surfaced in the shallow riffle below.

It was evening, and the high peaks were still rosy in the setting sun, when the otters reached the spot where the river empties into the Kootenai Lakes, cradled in the valley between ranks of giant spruce and ancient cottonwoods. They had been travelling nearly twenty-four hours, and both were hungry and ready for a period of relative inactivity. Proo climbed up onto a driftwood log to groom herself, while Kim investigated a log jam out where the ripples of the stream lost themselves on the mirror surface of the lake. His ears caught the sound of branches snapping, and he reared up on a log to look at a giant bull moose browsing among the willows at the foot of an avalanche track. Paying it no further attention, he humped slowly along the log to a sand spit sticking out into the lake. Here he rolled, and scrubbed his coat for a while before entering the water to dive under a floating pad of driftwood.

The flickering movement of a trout caught his eyes as it darted away, and a powerful twist of his body instantly sent him in pursuit. The fish turned, twisted and dodged, frantic to escape, but the otter followed its every move, slowly closing in until his teeth snapped shut on its back. Then he returned to the sand spit, climbed up on the log and proceeded to eat his catch.

Proo came to investigate, but was greeted by an ominous growl, which sent her back across the sand to the water. Her fishing trip took her a bit longer, but she was soon back on shore with another fat trout.

When they finished feeding, the otters travelled a short distance to a tangled heap of logs left by winter avalanches, and there, in a dark, dry cavern under the pile, they found a comfortable nest and slept.

In the morning they were off again, making a long circuit of the shoreline of the two lakes and the short swift section of river that joined them. It was a pristine, lovely place, teeming with fish and many other kinds of life. A family of fully grown harlequin ducks in drab juvenile and female plumage floated on the surface of the first lake, but the otters paid them scant attention. On the second lake, near the end where the river exited, there was a small beaver house built on the edge of a semi-floating island made of tangled grass braided into dwarf willow roots. The otters climbed up on its dome-shaped roof, examining its freshly plastered coating of mud and sniffing the musky-sweet smell of beavers before sliding back into the water.

Along the shore of the lake, Proo came to a place where a little spring flowed out of a wet carpet of moss growing at the feet of some big spruce. This miniature delta was fringed with emerald green watercress, which she sampled with relish before beginning to dig into the wet muck,

125

hauling up gobs of it with her front paws and rooting around in the blackened water with her nose. A movement under her paws triggered a quick plunge, and her teeth closed on a squirming frog that had buried itself in the silt under the little flow for the winter. She ate it and started digging for another. Behind her, Kim came out of the lake with a small trout in his jaws. The hunting was good in this place.

The Indian summer days were warm with a gentle chinook wind blowing down the valley off the Divide. The tops of the high peaks had a light frosting of new snow that was a silvery contrast to the golden larches just below timberline. The few cottonwoods along the lake shores were a brilliant yellow against the deep green of the conifers. Sometimes alone, more often together, the otters wandered the lakes, and up and down the river, exploring, feeding and frolicking. They were fat under their shining coats of rich brown.

One evening a thick, clammy fog settled down from the peaks, and the north wind came cold with snowflakes drifting on it. By morning the whole country was transformed into a snow-draped wilderness, and the lake surfaces were covered in lead-coloured slush. Somewhere up toward the summit of the Divide, a flock of Canada geese, trying to cross over the pass, lost their direction in the storm. They dropped lower, circling and honking. When they found themselves over the river, they doubled back along it to the lakes, where they landed near the island. Not long afterward a flock of several hundred mallards came flying low up the river and joined the geese. The place was suddenly alive with bird sounds.

Otters are naturally curious animals with a penchant for investigating everything around them, and Kim and Proo swam out for a look. Travelling under water, they surfaced here and there, sniffing and peering toward the raft of ducks

126

till they were within a few yards of them. Then Kim dove and slid up under a fat drake. He grabbed it by a foot and pulled it under so suddenly that it had time for no more than a short lifting of its wings and a cut-off squawk. Kim took it deep, released it, shifting his grip to its neck before it could move, and killed it with a swift crunch of his teeth. He surfaced to get air about fifty feet from shore, and towed it the rest of the way to the snowy beach.

Proo was not hungry, for she had just killed and eaten a trout, but she was feeling playful. Diving under the ducks, and looking up, she could see the outlines of them clustered on the surface, and she came up to nip one lightly. The hen mallard quacked in panicky alarm at this shocking attack by something from the depths, and jumped into the air to land with head held high a few feet away. Her sudden leap caused a slight ripple of concern among the ducks in her immediate vicinity, making a hole in the tightly crowded bottoms visible to Proo. She surfaced very briefly in the middle of the gap thus created and dived to repeat the manoeuvre. Again the duck of her choice leapt up in consternation, with an accompanying clatter of other wings. This sudden vanishing of outlines excited the otter so that she continued to nip and bump bottoms till the whole flock took to the air.

Proo surfaced to find herself surrounded by a broken tracery of slush where ducks had been. Only the geese remained in a close bunch by the edge of the island, so she turned her attention to them. Their reaction was more ponderous, but just as satisfying. After a couple of submarine sallies, however, sharp eyes quickly spotted her head as she came up for a look, and the geese climbed up onto the island, spoiling Proo's game. The ducks landed again after a couple of circles of the lakes, but Proo had lost interest. She swam away toward the outlet of the river, where she was shortly joined by Kim.

There the otters climbed up to the top of a steep slanting

slab of rock below a low waterfall to slide down, making a trough in the snow and ending in a plunge into the tumbling cauldron of a deep pool. Again and again they climbed, to repeat the tobogganing until their track was slick with ice from the water on their fur.

A big lynx crouched watching them, a few yards away under the wide spreading branches of a spruce, but the smell and the size of them, coupled with their strangeness, cooled his first inclination to attack. His muscles relaxed as he watched curiously until they left their game to disappear back upstream. Then he faded into the snowy forest in search of something more familiar to satisfy his hunger. A smart move — had he attacked them, the otters would have ganged up and drowned him.

The storm had been short, but the snow was a foot deep when the sun came out to light up the wintry wilderness. This transition between warm fall days and the first breaths of winter is a restless time of year among wild animals. On the few remaining bright, golden days the sun seems to kiss the earth with a cooling fervour, as though saying goodbye before the arrival of cold and deep snow.

There are deep valleys in the mountains running parallel to the daily passage of the sun. In these valleys the high flanking peaks hide the sunlight from December to March. Most of the bigger animals, particularly the cloven-hoofed ones, shun these places.

The bears escape winter's grip by going into dens for the cold months, and living off their fat in semi-hibernation. The beavers take refuge in their dome-shaped houses, feeding on the bark of willows, aspens and cottonwood stored in submerged piles under the ice. The winter birds, well insulated by thick plumage, endure the cold as they forage over wide areas. The pine squirrels build bulky nests of dry moss in the trees and live off caches of pine nuts, spruce and fir seeds and carefully dried mushrooms, sleeping during the sharp cold spells. The pine martens live by hunting the squirrels, just as the otters hunt and eat the aquatic life found under the armour of ice that covers the frozen lakes, ponds and streams.

Kim and Proo found an old, abandoned beaver run dug into the bank of the river between the lakes, and moved into it. Its mouth was deep under water, so they had quick access to the lakes and good fishing. Sometimes they swam up to the open water where the river came down swiftly into the lake. Occasionally, they made short journeys through the snow under the timber along the edge of the lakes, but as the loose fluffy blanket piled up, these trips were abandoned. Swimming under the ice was easier.

By February there was twelve feet of snow on the level, and because the sun had never shone during the cold months, it had remained a loose blanket. Now the sun was back, growing higher and stronger every day, and the snow began to settle. The otters could travel easily from one open hole in the river to another, but still there was small inducement for them to wander very far.

As warmer weather began to open the river, Proo was heavy with young, her usually sleek outline bulky and her temper short. One day her tolerance of Kim broke and, in a snarling fit of rage, she drove him out of the den so vigorously that he did not return. He burrowed down among the logs to take up residence in their old nest.

It was just pure luck that he was out fishing the day an avalanche cut loose high on the mountain slope above the lakes, and came roaring down, smashing into the log jam and tearing it apart, finally coming to rest with a great pile of snow extending half-way out into the upper lake. Its plunging weight broke the ice, and the snow mass displaced thousands of tons of water, the resulting wave inundating Proo's den and driving her out, where she found that the water level was up into the timber. When the flood subsided the snow was dirty with forest flotsam, and the ice of the lower lake was covered with water.

Kim swam around the snout of the snow-pile, inspecting this sudden change of landscape, and climbed up onto the great mound for a brief reconnaisance before taking to the water again. He swam through the lower lake into the river, heading for new country, leaving the place to Proo.

When she went back to it, her den was damp and cold, so unattractive that she abandoned it to search for better surroundings. There was an urgency to her looking as she travelled along the shoreline of the lower lake, poking her nose into every nook and cranny along the edge of the timber. Most of the land was still deep in snow, but on top of a steep-sided little gravel ridge near the river outlet, she came on a big, bleached-out cottonwood log lying in the midst of a thick growth of willows. It was forked at one end, and in the middle of the fork there was a round hole big enough to accommodate her. She found the interior of the hollow log lined with bits of rotten wood, dry and ideal for a hide.

When she came back to it from a fishing trip late that evening, she did not enter the log until she had made a circle all around it, sniffing and examining everything, to satisfy herself that nothing had intruded upon her new territory. Then she slipped through the hole, but even in the security of the hide she was restless, and came out again to poke aimlessly around as though in search of something. Finally she found a small patch of old dry grass along the rim of a bank, and proceeded to collect mouthfuls of it to carry back to her log. After several trips, her nest was arranged to her satisfaction, and she stretched out on her grassy bed.

That night her kits were born — four tiny, helpless little mites with eyes sealed shut. They squeaked and nuzzled as she licked them dry, until one by one they fastened onto a dug to nurse.

During these first hours after their birth, Proo was by

turns keenly on edge and alert to the slightest noise outside the log, and gently — even ecstatically — preoccupied with her new family. She licked them with soft caresses while they cuddled up close to her belly, secure and content in her warmth.

No longer was she a carefree wandering animal, for she spent no more time away from her hide than it took to feed. She did not play any more, but pursued fish with a swift, fierce concentration of purpose, anxious to be back with her family.

The kits developed quickly, and by warm weather they were trailing their mother to the lake, where they took to the water without hesitation, soon as much at home in it as she was. By June, the family was taking longer and longer expeditions away from the hide. Proo would lead and the kits would bring up the rear, the first one with its nose even with the end of Proo's tail, and the rest single-filing behind in close formation. As they followed undulations of the ground — up and over logs and rocks and around trees — they were an unbroken chain, moving in formation like a long brown ribbon.

In the lake, when Proo dived in pursuit of fish, they dipped under in an attempt to follow but their dives were very shallow.

When she reappeared, she usually had a trout crosswise in her mouth. After reaching shore and locating some suitable cover, she ate the head off her catch, leaving the kits to maul the rest of it while she dove back into the water after another.

One evening, when she took them back to the hide, she heard something moving and crackling among the willows near it. Rearing behind a patch of green fireweed to her full height, she found that the log had been rolled to one side. Behind it, a big grizzly was sniffing around in the brush. With a low growl of warning, she quickly led the kits back to the lake and they swam up toward its head. She took them into a big eddy in the river, close by the mouth of her old den, and dove. Quickly exploring the den, she came back out to the young ones, who were milling around, fighting to hold their position in the swirling current. Grasping a kit in her mouth, she dove back into the tunnel with a powerful twist of her muscular body, and deposited it inside, above waterline. Not wasting a motion, she repeated the manoeuvre until her family was all safely inside, then she took them up the tunnel to the small chamber hollowed out at the top. This place was not as dry as the log, but it was a good hide, located under the spreading roots of a giant spruce, and safe from any intrusion.

For a while, the kits required her help in the dive to and from the river, but it was not long before they learned to make it by themselves. The young otters grew fast, and by late summer they were swift powerful swimmers. Now the family was continually ranging and playing together, welded into a solid unit. Their lives seemed to be an unending game of follow-the-leader, with Proo as the leader. As closely as possible, the young ones copied her every move. They were diving now in pursuit of fish, though their enthusiasm surpassed their success. Even so, they came close enough to whet their zeal for more trying, and they revelled in the excitement.

One day in mid-July something new appeared by the lake — a tent pitched on the meadow by the beach at the lower end where the river exited. It was the camp of a doctor and his wife on their annual wilderness fishing trip into the Rockies. They were accompanied by their fox terrier.

The lady was not as keen about fishing as her husband, and spent a good deal of her time wandering about, watching birds and photographing flowers.

Proo became aware of them, when the sounds of supper preparation and the smell of campfire smoke alerted her, but she was not unduly alarmed, as she had encountered people and camps before. Like all wild mothers she was always cautious, and for a while she kept the kits close to the hide. They were a restless brood; their energy and enthusiasm difficult to contain for very long at a time. One morning they were causing Proo considerable anxiety by diving out of the tunnel one at a time, and finally she took them out to the upper lake.

On a sandbar by the log jam at the foot of the avalanche track, she began to dive for a trout, while the kits played on the sand among some big bleached logs. Proo had just surfaced a few feet from the shore with a fish in her jaws, when the lady and her dog came out of the timber fifty yards down wind from the otters, and immediately the dog caught their scent. He gave a sharp bark of excitement and streaked away, arriving among the kits before his mistress comprehended what was going on.

The fact that he suddenly found himself confronted by several small animals instead of one, confused him for an instant, which probably saved a life. His open jaws were just reaching for one of the kits, when Proo smashed into his side, and instantly the quiet was convulsed into a scene of utter bedlam, accompanied by snarls and hair-raising screeches, chilling in their utter savagery. Proo was attacking with a red-eyed intent to kill sparked to burning intensity by her mother-instinct to protect her young. The dog, though he was in excellent condition, young and strong, found himself up against a terror, bound in muscles like steel springs and with the speed of lightning.

They rolled and spun, locked together in a death battle. The otter's hide was tough and loose, so that no matter how or where the terrier grabbed her, she turned in her skin and nailed him with her teeth. Although wild with anger, she was fighting with a pattern; she was working him toward the water where she would have an overwhelming advantage.

But before they reached it, the lady arrived, screaming at the top of her lungs and waving a stick. With no thought of possible consequences, she waded into the mix-up, breaking her stick over the otter's back. Although mad with rage, the otter realized she was now outnumbered, and broke away to plunge into the lake and disappear. Her kits had long since gone, but she sensed that they were ahead of her, and she turned toward the hide.

Meanwhile the lady had gathered up her dog, and, with blood running over her clothes from a deep gash on its shoulder and a badly torn face and ear, she headed for camp. The good doctor had some sewing to do.

Proo gathered up her family and took them back into the hide. For a while there would be no problem keeping them there, for they were shaking with fright. As for her, she tingled with the pain of bites, but apart from a few punctures in her tough hide she was unhurt. Just the same, for a while she growled at every sound that came through thin spots on the tunnel's roof, and even at the kits when they jostled her as they nursed.

Next day the tent on the lakeshore had vanished, along with the people using it, but a few days later another appeared, and again Proo found herself sharing the lakes with people — a condition that made her nervous — and her discipline of the carefree kits became stricter.

She was restless, and one morning during a rain storm, she led the kits down into the river. This time, she did not turn back at the first falls, but continued downstream for several miles until the river emptied into Waterton Lakes.

The tourist season was at its height and there seemed to be people everywhere; the noise of power boats, large and small, assailed her ears during daylight hours, prompting her to hide with her family in any kind of available cover. At night, it was comparatively peaceful, a time for her to catch fish as she explored. The creeks coming down the steep mountain flanks into the main body of water were short, swift and small, for the most part offering no attraction. For a couple of days she explored a larger creek, fishing at its mouth and living in a log jam upstream near a waterfall, but even here, it was a constant worry, for people came and went along a trail close to the water.

At last, in the dark of night, her restlessness drove her to lead her family along the west shore of the main lake until she suddenly found herself on the edge of a well-lit town. Here the air was full of even more noise and strange smells, so she retreated back along the beach for a way and then struck out, swimming across the lake to the far side. She followed this shoreline, but before she had gone very far, it began to pinch in closer and closer to the town, where the shore was rocky and offered no cover, so she pointed her nose inland, climbing along the side of a rocky ridge.

Now, for the first time in her life, she was being driven hard in her search for cover — any kind of cover. As dawn paled the eastern sky, she came to the edge of a little marshy slough trapped among scrub aspens in a fold of the slope. Among some small trees she found a hide. After nursing the kits, she went foraging in the shallow water, but apart from a few frogs and snails, the place was barren.

That night she was on the move again, leading the kits up onto a height of land that jutted from the base of a mountain looming dark and high against the stars. An updraft of wind brought the welcome smell of much water to her nose, and she speeded up her descent toward it, with the kits in close formation at her heels. As they were crossing a bare rock rib in the starlight, the last young otter in the line was lagging a bit. Suddenly, on silent wings, a great horned owl dropped from the top of a snag to strike. The big bird would have been successful if its intended victim had not taken that moment to close the gap ahead of it. The owl found itself looking at what appeared to be a much bigger target, and checked itself momentarily, the flash of its wings alerting Proo. Instantly she presented the owl with a snarling target — open-jawed and formidable, with teeth bared — turning it away to find something easier to kill.

The scent of water turned out to be a lake along the base of a low, broken cliff, and Proo immediately went fishing, but with no success, for here the water dropped sheer away to great, gloomy depths. After a couple of fruitless dives, she continued down the lake shore at a steady pace. Dawn was just breaking when she led her family into the top of a river.

At the first big pool below the lake, she dove and found it teeming with fish. She quickly killed a heavy whitefish, which was torn apart and eaten ravenously. Then they all rolled and scrubbed themselves on the damp shingle of fine gravel and sand, before setting out again downriver. As they passed through some grass on the edge of a stagnant backwater pool, Proo came on a garter snake. Hardly breaking her stride, she grabbed it by the head, killed it with one crunch, then, trailing its body to one side like a bit of rope, proceeded to eat it by jerking it into her mouth in munching gulps accompanied by gusty growls as the kits took turns trying to fasten onto the trailing end. They got no part of this delicacy, and shortly the still wiggling tail disappeared down her throat.

A quarter mile below, they were under a giant old ruin of a cottonwood. It had once been forked twenty feet from the ground, but a windstorm had broken off one fork, leaving a splintered blaze on the trunk. A hole showed in the scar. The tree was still alive, with the top of the remaining portion covered with green leaves. At its base it looked like any other big cottonwood, but between the forking bosses of two heavy roots, among a tangle of greenery, Proo poked her nose into a hole. She slid into it, and found herself in a perfect hide inside the hollow trunk, with a little patch of blue sky showing through the scar high overhead.

136

But the day had scarcely started when she became aware of people, for this stretch of the river was a favourite place for fishermen. Proo had no way of knowing that they posed no threat inside the park. Her experience with the dog had left its imprint, so she remained in a constant state of nervousness all day, hearing voices, sniffing the alien smell of humans, and aware of the crunching vibrations of footsteps.

As soon as it was dark, she returned to the river with her family, continuing her search for a haven of peace and quiet, a quest that had taken on an aura of urgency. Her way was tortuous, following the shore of the stream and two adjoining lakes, although it did not take them far across the country. During the second night after she had entered this river, she came to a muddy-bottomed creek flowing from the south into one of the lakes, and followed it up through a heavy growth of willows and aspens to where a big beaver dam blocked the stream. This dam was the first of many built like a series of steps, each one with a pond above it.

Some were old constructions surrounded by bleached stumps and snags midst tangles of deadfall, the ponds dotted with water-killed trees, still standing, bleached out by weather, white as bone. In the newer ones some of the trees were still green. It was a wilderness of water, tangled timber and brush engineered with incredible ingenuity to stop water from running downhill. There was no obvious pattern to the dams and ponds, yet it was effective, for the stream was under almost complete control. No flood could wash out this marvelous series of mud and stick constructions; high water merely widened the ponds, spreading them out into the surrounding timber, to search out hollows and lie there till the excess water slowly drained off.

It was a beaver city laced with a network of canals, underground tunnels and dams, with ponds surrounding the domes of their houses. The ponds teemed with life: fish, mainly suckers; wild ducks, geese and other wildfowl which used the acres of water and the diversity of ideal cover; mink and muskrats which had joined the beaver hosts. The warm water was full of vegetation which supported masses of aquatic insect larvae and crustaceans, all part of an intricate and abundant food chain. The trees and brush along the perimeters were alive with birds, large and small, from eagles to hummingbirds. For Proo and her family it was like discovering heaven.

The otters' arrival made hardly a ripple on the surface of this complex life system of water and forest, yet they wrote a paragraph of history, for no other otters had made tracks along this stream for more than half a century.

Almost instantly, Proo's brood became avid fishermen. When they came up over the top of the first dam at dawn and dived into the pond, they found themselves in the middle of a school of suckers darting hither and yon like a cloud of blunt-nosed projectiles. Proo immediately fastened her teeth in one, swam back to the dam and proceeded to eat, but her kits excitedly milled around as though unable to believe what they were seeing. They dived again and again, and although they were anything but skilful, there was no way they could miss. In a short while all five otters were lined up along the top of the dam, busily chewing on their catches; the kits occasionally declaring their territorial rights by glaring at each other and growling fiercely in comical threats. As they finished their fish, they dove back to catch more, eating till they bulged, and then catching even more for the sheer excitement of it. Proo sat hunched in the warmth of the rising sun, grooming herself, and one by one the kits left their sport to join her.

Again she led the way upstream over one dam after another, cruising among flooded trees, exploring. There were a thousand hides to choose from here; leafy bowers deep with shade, caverns under tangled logs, and various holes and hollows under overhanging banks. It was a jungle — green and intertwined with lush growth — where the otters blended and lost themselves in the tangled wilderness of water and timber. The maze of beaver waterways offered a host of diversions for the curious otters, to say nothing of an abundance of feed. Here they could move freely without encountering humans, for, although this place was within a few miles of busy highways leading into the park, no people ventured into this tangle in the middle of a trackless aspen forest. It was truly wild, but not always so quiet.

One evening, on the tail of an oppressively hot, close afternoon, Proo and her family emerged from under some tall, leafy cow cabbage plants to play and dive amongst some half-submerged logs. A great towering cloud rolled in over the western mountains, its undulating rim looking as white and hard as carved ivory, backlit by the sun it had blotted out. It was moving fast, and the deepening gloom was suddenly torn by jagged shafts of lightning. Thunder rolled like giant drums, shattering the quiet, echoing and banging off the mountain slopes.

A splattering of raindrops dotted the surface of the pond where the otters played. The steady undertone of a rushing roar that accompanied the storm rose to a sudden climax as hailstones suddenly descended with a thunderous pelting that drowned out all but the loudest blasts of thunder.

Proo immediately led her family in search of shelter, the arrival of the hail giving her little time for choice. Some of the stones were as big as duck eggs, and most were over half an inch in diameter, so the danger of injury to the kits was very real. Although she had never experienced anything like this, she sensed the peril and took the first shelter she found. It was a wedge-shaped cavity under the rotten butt of a big dead log lying on the bank.

She led the way into it in a rush, followed closely by the kits, each one crowding up and overlapping the one in front till the whole family was stuffed into the hole — all except the rump and tail of the last one in line. This shelter, that would easily have held all five otters a month before, could now contain only four and a half. The protruding one got a big hailstone squarely on the root of its tail, which made it squeal and claw its way desperately ahead to dislodge the otter in front of it. It in turn clawed its way forward to dislodge another, which in turn found *its* rear exposed, and in short order the process was repeated. So it was only a matter of time before Proo found herself at the rear of her brood with her hindquarters exposed to the elements. She growled and grumbled about it, but endured.

The hailstorm ended as quickly as it had begun, revealing the pond grey with floating ice, the trees half denuded of their leaves and the ground herbage pounded flat. The surface of the earth was white with a four-inch coating of hailstones. The otters took to the water again, unmindful of its sudden chill, to swim upstream.

Here and there dead ducks floated on the surface; it was their moulting season, so the storm had caught them without the usual protection of thick plumage. A bull moose lay inert, half submerged in the water, killed by lightning as he had waded across looking for shelter. A crippled red-tailed hawk clung to its perch on a branch on a cottonwood, a drooping wing proclaiming a broken bone that condemned it to a slow death. A great horned owl shook itself, trying to dry its bedraggled feathers, squeaking querulously as it looked down from a more sheltered perch on another big tree. The storm had been cruel to the wild ones. Only the beavers, muskrats, mink and otters escaped unscathed in the corridor cut by the hail, and as darkness came down these were out swimming and feeding as always.

Through late summer and early fall, the otter family, the only ones of their kind living there, revelled in the wild abundance of the valley hidden away among the forested hills. But one morning, as they played on a slide over the water sluiceway of a big dam, Proo discovered the scent of another otter. She was instantly alert and watchful, as if the scent stirred old memories. Suddenly she saw the head and neck of a big otter thrust up out of the water of the pond below, as it watched the kits tobogganing down the slide. With a fluid motion, quick as a flicker of light, Proo launched herself in a long dive down over the dam, entering the water with scarcely a splash to go streaking out towards the visitor. Surfacing, she lifted her head and forequarters high to look, just as the other otter did the same, and they hissed at each other as they began to circle.

It was Kim, recently arrived over a height of land separating this creek from another, a tributary of the Belly River, where he had spent the summer. After some preliminary skirmishing and introduction, both otters began to play — a beautiful, powerfully smooth water ballet, trading the roles of pursuer and pursued, ecstatic after a long separation.

But there were limits to Proo's permissiveness with Kim, for she would not allow him to approach the kits too closely. They, in turn, were shy, never having known another adult otter but their mother. However, otters are naturally very sociable animals, and a kind of loose family association developed between Kim, Proo and the kits. While he obviously welcomed the fraternization with his own kind, he was much more restless than they were, often disappearing for days on some trip beyond the drainage of the creek.

By winter the young otters were almost totally self-sufficient, pursuing their own prey, but still maintaining their close ties with their mother, following at her heels wherever she went.

Except where the ponds were kept open by big springs or fast water the ice and snow that covered them was marked by the distinctive trails of the otters. This was not like the deep snow country of their birth; it was much more subject to strong, warm chinook winds blowing from the mountains. Cold spells and snow storms were interspersed with periods of wild wind that stirred up ground blizzards so thick that the air seemed to be a moving river of the white stuff in unsheltered places. Tracks would be wiped out within minutes, then a new fall would offer a clean page on which all the animals could write the stories of their passing — repetitious, yet often dramatic in its detail.

The otters mainly fed on fish, sometimes eating their catches in caverns under the ice caused by a lowering of the water level, but more often sitting on the ice by an open hole. For the most part their scats glistened with fish scales; occasionally they showed fur from muskrats; and sometimes they were green with vegetation picked up as they foraged among underwater aquatic gardens for the swarms of freshwater shrimp found there.

Late one evening in February, as a three-quarter moon flashed periodically through fast drifting clouds, Proo led the way down the creek and past the lowest dam for the first time since the otters had arrived in the valley. When she reached the broad expanse of frozen lake at the creek, she led the way out across the wind-polished ice. Here the young otters revelled, at first in a thoroughly disorganized mix-up of rolling and sliding, but then following her lead in a rhythmic pattern of two loping jumps and a long slide. In their usual close-coupled line they went in step, a routine that carried them rapidly across the slippery surface.

Proo led them thus across the lake to the spot where the river flowed out of it, and there they plunged into an open hole at the top of a swift riffle, and, taking advantage of air pockets under the ice to breath, they continued on downstream. The fast water of a rapids was exciting but not the least frightening, for the otters were in their element, ecstatic with the exhilaration of the buffeting water adding to their speed.

They came to the mouth of a creek that ran down a little valley from the north and into the river, and Proo pointed her nose up it. This slowed their travelling down some, though they continued at a steady pace, sometimes on top of the ice and sometimes under it.

Late the next afternoon I found otter tracks far from the haven of the park, in the midst of a wilderness of beaver dams built below a series of big artesian springs — the headwaters of the creek. As I stood among some willows, examining the unusual trail on a skiff of new snow covering the ice over a frozen channel, a flicker of movement on top of a spillway on a dam a few yards upstream caught my eye. Five otters appeared and slid down the half-frozen chute to disappear under the ice. About a minute later, they appeared again on top of the dam below, obviously heading down the creek.

The lives of all animals are fraught with risk from the moment they are born, regardless of where they live, but when furbearers like otters leave the shelter of a national park to come into a settled area, they are exposed to far greater dangers. For otters have a bounty on them; not a price on their heads, but on the rich coats they wear. Even though otters are extremely rare, they enjoyed no protection in regulation — perhaps because they were thought to be non-existent in this region. As I stood looking after them, I wondered what their fate would be, for there were trappers working this part of the country.

Perhaps it was pure luck, maybe it was because their visits to the various creeks were so irregular, or possibly they spent most of their time in the park; but somehow they missed getting into trouble that year.

One spring morning, after the ice had gone out and the creek was boiling with melt-water, I stood on the edge of a bank behind a fringe of willows, and looked down into a swirling pool flecked with foam and bubbles eddying in the current. The otter family was playing there with a chunk of old dry horse manure one of them had apparently rolled down from the bank. It floated as buoyantly as a cork, and they were taking turns swimming under it and flipping it into the air, pushing it under and passing it back and forth like players in a game of water polo. It was a fascinating and very rare opportunity to observe an exhibition of otters' innate love of play, an inborn characteristic which sometimes leads them to astonishing innovations. As they are very shy, lovers of seclusion, and tremendous travellers fond of heavy cover, their games are not often witnessed except in the tracks they leave. My privilege was something to cherish, and I watched till their improvised ball got so wet it disintegrated, and the otters disappeared, still unaware of their audience.

Several times that summer, while fishing for trout along the creeks and the river both in and out of the park, I found their tracks. Because they were still travelling as a family unit, their trail was easy to see. Only the male travelled alone, though on occasion he joined them.

By fall, the young otters were almost fully grown, and every time I saw their sign I wondered again what was in store for them. What fate would be their lot as they led this idyllic life along the waterways at the foot of the Rockies? As it turned out, there was to be a drastic change.

When winter came again, the moccasin telegraph carried the news of a trapper getting a big otter in one of his sets. His friends came from all around to see this marvelous pelt, all of five feet long from the nose to the tip of the tail. He kept it hung in a conspicuous place in a lean-to adjoining his cabin, where he often stood to gaze at it in admiration.

He was something of a romantic, and was heard to say as he showed it to a friend, "There you hang, all glistenin' and gleamin'! You'll look mighty handsome hung around some fine lady's shoulders."

His first success prompted further efforts, and Proo's family fell victim to his artfully set traps, one by one. It is unlikely she experienced grief, only a sense of loss and loneliness, but for certain sure she developed cunning where traps were concerned. When greening-up time came again and her fur was sunburnt and worthless, I found her tracks once more, where I had first encountered them the year before, along the upper reaches of the creek outside the park. It was a fleeting contact I would not often experience again.

All that following summer and fall I watched for her tracks, but her sign was scarce, appearing at long intervals over a very wide area.

Now there was little sign of play along her trails, for her life seemed to be an endless, restless searching for another of her kind. Near the end of the tourist season, the captain of the big launch that plied the upper Waterton saw an otter on a driftwood log on shore near the mouth of the Kootenai River. It was likely Proo retracing her old trail back up to Kootenai Lakes.

Where did she go? Who knows? No sign of any otter have ever been reported again along the foot of the mountains. Perhaps when the larches were turning gold once more, she retraced her old trail back up over the pass across the spine of the Rockies and down into the country where she was born. Maybe there she was joined by another otter to mate again, and raise other families along the wild upper reaches of the Flathead River.

She did not know it, but she had contributed something very special to my life. Sometimes I recall with nostalgia those months of reading track stories in snow and silty mud, and I cannot help wondering what became of her.

Kleo

From high up, looking down along its spine, the north ridge of the Horn was warm with the coppery red reflection of a fiery sunset on its western flank, and to the east it was deep in shadow, facing the purple tints of twilight touching the rim of the prairie eighty miles or so away. The top of the ridge was serrated unevenly, like the back of some ancient prehistoric monster lying asleep against the side of the peak; the humps capped by weathered turrets, rough-hewn by countless years of weather, like castle ruins so old they only hinted at shapes once known. It was cool and very still, the quiet a poignant thing as the mountains and everything in them paused in contemplation of the blazing sky.

Out of nowhere, skylined on the highest point, there came a big, red-gold tom cougar. He stalked along with a peculiar grace known only to the cat kingdom, and upon reaching the crest, he stopped. He slowly swept his gaze across the slope toward the forked canyons of Pine Creek, his eyes glowing a blazing yellow, hot orbs betraying his bad temper, a frame of mind accented by the twitching end of his long tail.

For Kleo was a very angry cat. As he walked across the mountains, waving his tail wildly in reminiscence of romance lost, he tingled and burned from a score of wounds inflicted on his tough hide by the claws and teeth of a successful rival.

Two nights before, as he had come down a slope through a tangled mess of wind-tortured timber, he had run head-on into the galvanizing scent of a female coming into heat. Immediately he had followed his nose on down into a canyon, where he found her busy raking flotsam over what was left of a mountain goat that she had killed, near the foot of a waterfall, a high ribbon of water swaying and undulating like a silvery rope in the breeze.

The moon was up, several days off the full, a bit flat on one side as though it had run into something in a careless moment, but shedding a pale, ghostly light as Kleo had oozed down across the broken rocks to within twenty steps of the lioness. He had announced himself with a short call, sounding somewhat like a musical burp, and she had whirled around to face him like a coiled spring ready to unwind, answering him with a very unlovely snarl. It was not encouraging. Even though he was a full grown cat, all of eight feet from tip to tip, she was bigger. He was young and she looked formidable to him but she smelled very good; the air was full of promise, prompting Kleo to be patient even though he trembled with desire.

He had crouched absolutely motionless, like a dramatic carving of a mountain lion, watching her as she relaxed and continued with the burial of her kill. When she had arranged it to her satisfaction, she had stepped back to take a drink from the pool at the bottom of the falls, then climbed up past her claim to dig a hole in the loose shale and urinate. After covering everything with fastidious care, in the way of all cats, she had leapt up on top of a boulder, giving him another snarl, composed herself, and proceeded to lick her paws and scrub her face.

Upon finishing her toilet, she had climbed straight up the mountain, pausing at the foot of the broken cliffs above to look back, as though daring him to even glance toward her cache. Kleo couldn't have possibly cared less about food, his mind was on one track and that ran directly to her. So when she had moved up, climbing the massive staircase of broken ledges at one side of the falls with infinite elegance, he had followed at a discreet distance, as though a string fastened his nose to the slightly curling end of her long tail.

So it had gone for the rest of the night and most of the next day, their trail following a crazy pattern that went nowhere in particular; all over the side of the mountain, in and out, around and over a succession of obstacles, so steep in places that it would have given a goat some pause for thought before he moved a foot. As a matter of fact, several goats had observed this impending romance with such extreme misgivings, that they had hoisted their ridiculous excuses for tails straight up and quit the mountain.

During the course of this round of exercise, the female had eventually led the way back down to her kill where she had fed again, after threatening Kleo with murder if he dared step into the invisible circle she had drawn around it.

Upon finishing her feed and reburying her cache, she had led the way, by a circuitous route, along the flank of the canyon into a grove of wind-twisted pines, where she had finally stopped and lain down in a shady grotto, cool under the late afternoon sun. Very carefully and with great patience, Kleo had worked in closer and closer, his whiskers occasionally vibrating to the accompaniment of faint chirps. Her ugly snarls had gradually lost their menace, and she had finally allowed him to gently lick her face. Very gradually, exercising enormous diplomacy, he had finally manoeuvred himself into a position where his front paws were about even with the root of her tail, his body parallel with hers and facing the same way. The long-promised moment was about to be reached; Kleo was on the verge of taking one more step to put him astride her back.

But — as though appearing out of the bowels of the earth — a huge tom cougar had stepped onto a log a few yards up the slope. For a long moment everything had frozen, the atmosphere saturated with a promise of riot. Kleo had lit the fuse with a squall that sounded something like a high-speed saw biting into a hard knot, and an explosion of a charge that had taken him to the intruder in three huge bounds. They had tangled in a frightful mix-up of teeth and claws. Rolling over and over in a fast-moving ball of fur and muscles, down the slope they had gone, banging into trees, breaking off snags and tearing up the forest floor, in a battle smoking with rage and the desire to kill.

What Kleo had lacked in experience, he had made up for in the youthful enthusiasm to wipe out this brigand who dared intrude into his territory at such a moment. But his adversary was an old hand, scarred by many battles; although momentarily taken aback by the savagery and swiftness of the attack, he had rallied. Every move he had made had been backed with purpose and deadly intent. It had been a no-holds-barred fight where second prize could have been severe injury or even death.

Kleo had found himself up against a devil; a giant who not only outweighed him, but who had muscles as hard as steel, and teeth and claws that cut and tore his hide every time they connected. No cat is long-winded enough to carry on a fight of such speed and storm for very long, and too soon Kleo's lungs had run out of oxygen. To his distress, self-preservation won out over procreation, and, with a screech of rage and frustration, he had suddenly torn free to dash away down the mountain. The bigger male had followed him for a way, but he had soon left, for his wind was also running short. He had stood watching Kleo go, his tail waving angrily back and forth and his face a mask of sheer ferocity, blood dripping from a cut across his nose.

Kleo had been beaten and he knew it, but that didn't cool his anger any. A drink at the creek in the canyon bottom, followed by a session of licking his wounds had not damped it either. So when he appeared on the crest of the broken castle at sunset, he was still seething and boiling, a very angry cougar — so furious, in fact, that he was talking to himself. He continued the soliloquy as he moved down the opposite side of the ridge, his waving tail signalling his rage.

To add to the discomfort of his smarting wounds, he was suddenly ravenously hungry, for he hadn't eaten anything for most of two days. In this frame of mind, his judgement wasn't very good when he ran into a porcupine chewing on the bark of a white scrub pine amongst a clutter of branches near the ground. It was a situation calling for skill and discretion, but Kleo wasn't charged with such virtues at the moment, so with more bravery than brains, he reached out a paw and proceeded to haul out the porky.

This was a grave mistake, for although the porcupine died almost instantly, his memory was to linger on for some time. Kleo's right front paw and the inside of his foreleg were liberally stabbed by over a hundred quills, their stiff barbed points deeply embedded. At first he paid them little heed, as he chewed away at the unprotected, soft underbelly of his victim, muttering and growling to himself in cougar profanity. When he tried to use the wounded paw to clean his face upon finishing his feed, however, he found it paining excruciatingly. He nipped and licked, working on the quills, but the more he tried to get them out, the farther they penetrated, and he only succeeded in breaking some off.

When he started to travel again, he was one very sorry cat, miserable and crippled. There is nothing that throws a feline off balance like any kind of severe injury, and Kleo was one step off being immobilized.

Among all the big cats, for that matter among all the bigger predators of the world, the cougar is one of nature's most efficient killers, matched only by a distant cousin, the African cheetah. A big cougar can kill a full grown elk or moose. They take ordinary deer with all the ease employed by a common house cat killing a mouse. Cougars are magnificently conditioned animals with every nerve and muscle tuned perfectly for quick killing. To such an animal, a paw full of porcupine quills is a disaster.

Travelling on three legs, Kleo was next to harmless, and the farther he went the worse it got; his paw swelled to twice its normal size, throbbing with excruciating pain even when he rested. Soon he was starving, for in the next two days all he managed to capture were a few mice and a half-grown rabbit. At one point he crept out on a big dead aspen log overhanging a beaver pond in an attempt to catch a duck that was feeding in some tall slough grass, but the log broke under his weight and all he got was wet.

That night he hobbled a couple of miles down a creek to suddenly find himself in a ranch yard. He stood, screened by tall grass near the outside corner of a rail fence, observing this alien scene, too miserable to even sniff or growl at its strangeness, when something moving caught his attention. It was another cat — a black and white mother barn cat coming back from a hunt. She was carrying a young rabbit half as big as herself for her brood of kittens cached under a manger in the barn.

She had been lucky in her foraging but now her good fortune ran out as her way brought her within six feet of Kleo's nose. Acting on reflex, without enquiring about identity or protocol, he simply jumped on her, cut off her squall of terror abruptly with a powerful crunch of his jaws, and proceeded to eat her — skin, bones, rabbit and all — without even pausing to lick his chops. He felt some better.

Silent as a shadow in spite of his gimpy leg, Kleo circled

the buildings looking for a suitable place to hide, for he was tired. His way took him across the creek, where he took a drink, then through a narrow band of thick willows, and up a bank under some big cottonwoods.

There, under the spreading branches of a big tree, he came upon an old truck; a derelict sinking on its rims in the tall grass of a meadow back of the corrals. It had been there a long time; spots of rust showed through its paint, and the window of the cab door on the side next to the creek was broken, offering an inviting hole. After circling around it a couple of times, examining its strangeness, Kleo reared up and peered through the gap left by the absence of the window, and finding it attractive, he jumped in. It was something like a cave, though its furnishings were most unusual. What was left of the seat cushions was soft, so he curled up and proceeded to go to sleep.

Strange noises roused him early in the morning, as the sun flooded the meadow and buildings with light. Kleo sat in the middle of the seat looking out through the windshield at surroundings the like of which he had never seen before; people and animals moving around, accompanied by sounds alien to his ears. But with typical cat-like deference to his injuries, and an awareness of a good hide if he kept absolutely still, he used his instincts and stayed put, without a thought of taking to his heels. Something told him that this place — close to water and providing shelter — was just what a crippled cougar needed, so he composed himself, even napping occasionally throughout the day.

Intermittently, he licked his festered, swollen paw and leg. No quills now showed, for porcupine quills always work their barbed points deeper and deeper into the flesh. Once when thirst moved him, he took advantage of the shadows and deep grass to slip out to the creek for a drink, but immediately returned to his hide-out.

When deep dusk came, and the sounds around the

153

buildings had subsided for the night, he emerged, hungry again, to wander down along the creek. A quarter of a mile away, where trees fringed the edge of a big alfalfa field, he spotted a herd of deer grazing, and immediately tensed in anticipation of a stealthy stalk, forgetting all about his sore paw. But at his first step he was quickly reminded of it, and stood angrily watching them, the tip of his tail switching. As far as he was concerned, the deer might as well have been grazing on the near slope of the moon.

For a while he poked around looking for something smaller, but he had no luck in that direction either, and for a very good reason. This ranch had a most unusual population of cats, the rancher and his wife being inordinately fond of them. Drowning batches of kittens was something that they just couldn't bring themselves to do, consequently there was a plethora of cats — dozens of them — inbred and half-starved, every colour of the rainbow, and with the exeption of four or five pets allowed to stay in the house, all of them almost continually hungry. Thus there were no mice or any other kind of small game within a considerable distance of the ranch buildings. Even the song-birds that managed to survive in the trees did so by exercise of extreme caution whenever they came to the ground. It was a place completely dominated by cats. Now Kleo's presence added a subtle disharmony to the general picture.

He returned to the fence corner where he had murdered his distant cousin the previous night, and moonlight bathed the yard in its pale glow as he stood camouflaged in the long grass in hope of a repeat opportunity. The place was strategically excellent, for it wasn't long before an orange tomcat, an old battle-scarred sexpot, the father of countless kittens (which he sometimes killed and ate when their mothers weren't looking), came sneaking along the rail fence heading for some distant hunting ground. All unaware of his impending doom, he came right up to Kleo's nose, and was dispatched with lightning swiftness. Kleo carried his catch into a willow thicket by the creek and ate it with gusto, even though it was extraordinarily tough. The repast whetted his appetite for more, so he went back to his stand, and by the time the first pale streaks of dawn gently fingered the eastern sky and the tops of the mountains, he had killed and eaten two more, orphaning another batch of kittens in the process. He then took another big drink and retired to his hide in the truck.

While the hunting was good, even though highly unorthodox, Kleo did not exactly bask on the fat of the land. His inroads on the ranch cats were sufficient to keep him alive, but he was gaunt and his fur had lost its sheen. However, his wounded foot was losing most of its swelling as his system absorbed the shafts of the quills and began to cover the insoluble points that lay flat against the bones in scar tissue. The fast decreasing cat population and his improving health were converging on a collision course, and something was bound to happen.

The rancher and his family were aware of the disappearance of their beloved felines, but the cause of their melting away was for some time a complete mystery. Nor were the two ranch dogs much help, for they were completely conditioned to the cat tribe. Early indulgence in the usual cat-and-dog mix-ups had resulted in punishment, causing them to ignore the cats almost completely. They became aware of Kleo shortly after he arrived, but after a few half-hearted barking sessions at night, they included him in the general cat-chasing taboo. So, for a while, Kleo enjoyed all the privacy of a veritable ghost.

One day the ten-year-old daughter of the family was out for a barefooted wade along the creek, playing in the delightfully cool water and overturning rocks to observe with fascination the wiggly creatures thus revealed. When she came to a point opposite the truck, for no particular reason

155

she went up to it, and climbed over the tailgate into the box. Idly, she went forward to the cab and peered into it through its rear window to find herself practically nose-to-nose with a huge cat. For a long, breath-catching moment both child and animal were frozen, then both broke and ran — the child on flying feet for the house, and Kleo out the window into the brush along the creek.

When the girl reached her father, who was working on a tractor in the yard, he could not make head or tail of what she was trying to tell him for several minutes, but when she calmed down enough to become reasonably articulate, he got his rifle and went with her to investigate. Of course, Kleo was long gone, but a few of his hairs clung to the nest on the truck seat, and then they located a big fresh track on some wet sand by the creek, further verifying her story. That find set off a chain of events that were to have some unusual, even traumatic consequences for the cougar.

Of course Kleo had no way of knowing this, or he would never have stopped travelling till he was on the other side of a large mountain. Sheer mischance had brought about a rare change of environment which he had used to bridge a painful period of his life. His indiscretion with the porcupine was nothing but a wave of the hand of fate, but the gesturing of that hand had not stopped.

Now that his foot was healing, and the hide in the truck was no longer secret, he was on the move, wandering down the creek toward its confluence with the river. It was too hot for travelling far, so he stretched out in the deep shade under some big cottonwoods, waiting for the cool of night. Like all his kind, he was a mostly nocturnal animal.

At first star-shine, he left the grove. The capricious finger of fate was beckoning, and he had not gone far when his trail took him back to the edge of the hay field just in time to see four yearling whitetail deer come frolicking out of the heavy cover into the open. There they began to gallop in a patternless kind of romp in the pleasantly cool evening air — and pure luck brought one of them within two short jumps of Kleo, flattened out in the tall growth. The little deer was looking away when Kleo landed on it, his teeth coming together in its fragile neck, and his great hooked claws clinching into its head and back. Its death was almost instant, and for the first time in weeks, Kleo had an ample supply of fresh, warm venison. He fed till his belly bulged, rolled on his back nearby, and snoozed, then roused himself to feed again.

As morning light came, he cached his kill under grass and raked-up forest debris, and left. It was quiet as he padded off through the timber. Suddenly, from somewhere back up the creek toward the ranch buildings, came the strange, long-drawn bawling of a hound, shortly joined by that of another. For a few moments he stopped, cocking his ears curiously. There was something ominous about that sound, and when he started travelling again, he was going at a lope.

On his backtrail, not far from his bed of the previous afternoon, a man held back on the leashes of two big blue-tick hounds as they slowly worked out the scent still clinging to the damp growth under the big cottonwoods. He was a famous predator hunter, called to take care of a cougar with an appetite for house cats; a mountain lion that chose to hole up in an old truck, and let a little girl come right up to him before running away. The rancher had correctly guessed that the presence of the cougar was somehow linked with the disappearance of the cats, and had telephoned the hunter, who had driven most of the night, his dogs riding in an enclosed box in the back of the truck. Upon reaching the ranch, it had not taken him long to pick up the cougar's trail. Now he held the hounds back on their leases while they worked out the track as far as the deer kill, and there they went wild with excitement, filling the clear morning air with their steady baying. When he slipped their leashes, they shot away,

157

bawling their heads off, their tails jerking and their big ears flying.

Kleo heard the uproar behind him and put on speed, but a belly full of meat and a tender foot slowed his running, and in no time the dogs were ravening at his heels. In something of a panic he leapt up the trunk of the first big tree that he came to — an old cottonwood with its top broken off. It was a short dead-end escape route that put him only about twice his length above the leaping hounds, their nerve-shattering racket keeping him there. Kleo flattened his ears at the bedlam and bared his formidable teeth in a snarl of anger mixed with not a little fear.

The hunter arrived, and stood looking up at the big cougar. Many times in similar circunstances, he had lifted a rifle to shoot the treed cat, but he had something else in mind for this one. He was not even carrying a gun. While he stood there sizing up the situation, he was joined by the rancher, who arrived on horseback, slipping out of the saddle and drawing his rifle from its scabbard in the same motion.

"We won't need the rifle," the hunter said. "Get your rope. I want this fellow alive. He don't know it yet, but he's going to be a movie star."

Kleo watched from his perch, flattened out in a crouch, and tensed as though about to jump, as the hunter walked slowly to his dogs. But he hesitated, perhaps because his foot was hurting, and the man snapped leashes onto the collars of the dogs to haul them back and tie them to a couple of small trees.

The hunter then slipped out of the shoulder straps of his small pack, and proceeded to take out a lariat and several shorter pieces of rope. As he carefully coiled the lariat, and arranged the short, noosed, tie ropes by tucking them under his belt, he softly gave instructions. He was cooly unhurried, moving smoothly as he stepped toward the foot of the tree. Some tall fireweeds interfered with the loop trailing in his hands, so he deliberately tramped them flat. Then, with a long step forward and a lightning fast flick of his wrist, he shot the loop toward its mark.

So quick it was hard to follow with the eye, Kleo reached out a paw and batted the rope to one side. Again, his muscles bunched under his hide as though he was getting set to jump, but again he hesitated.

"Easy, cat," intoned the hunter, as he recoiled the rope. Then he instructed the rancher, "This time when I get set to throw, toss your hat out to one side of the tree."

Again he stepped forward with wrist cocked; this time that hat went sailing out. The cougar's eyes were fastened on the hat when the rope struck to snap shut around his neck. The next instant, he jumped. The tightening rope threw him in a twisting somersault, but his feet were under him when he landed with a jarring thump, facing the man at the other end of it. Before the cat could move, the rope was around a tree. Every time he left the ground, the hunter dragged him toward the tree, until he was jammed up against its trunk, half-choked, but still snarling and fighting. The scene was one of bedlam, as the dogs yipped and bawled, turning handsprings at the end of their leashes. The rancher's lariat came into play, its loop snapping shut around the cougar's hind feet, and Kleo found himself stretched out, helpless to do much more than squirm and snarl.

Moving quickly, the hunter tied his rope around the tree, and then taking one of the short ones from his belt, he stepped in close to snare one front paw. A half hitch flickered around the other and they were drawn together to be tied securely, immobilizing the dangerous, hooked claws. Pulling a short, stout stick from his hip pocket, he thrust it into the cougar's open mouth crosswise, and when the raging animal bit down on it, another short rope noosed its projecting end, to be quickly wrapped in a figure eight

159

design around the cat's nose and jaw, effectively muzzling him. When the remaining tie rope was used on his hind feet, Kleo was absolutely helpless, only his eyes giving away his anger and fear — they gleamed like hot, green-gold coals.

Later that morning, when his truck rolled out of the rancher's gate onto the highway, the hunter was whistling. Beside him the dogs sat looking out through the windshield, their tongues lolling. Behind them in the dog box, Kleo lay panting, still securely tied and feeling the wheels rolling under him. The man felt particularly satisfied for he had had a standing order for a cougar with a big Hollywood motion picture company that was presently located in the mountains about one hundred and fifty miles to the north. Pointing the truck that way, he bore down on the gas pedal.

Kleo was suffering acutely from heat and thirst, his whole body throbbing and painfully cramped by the binding ropes. The unaccustomed sound and vibrations of the truck seemed to go on forever, clawing at his consciousness in an endless grinding nightmare. After what seemed a very long time, the truck slowed and finally stopped; the back door of the box opened letting in a blinding flood of sunlight. Without making a move to fight or struggle in any way, Kleo felt himself being dragged out and picked up bodily to be carried a ways and set down. The thongs binding him were removed, but for a while he just lay there, reaching for breath, unable to comprehend that he was free. When something tugged his tail, he came to his feet, glanced back at the men standing behind him, and leapt away, promptly running into the ungiving barrier of a steel link fence. He swerved clumsily in another direction and collided with the steel barrier again. Kleo was confused and frightened, and it took him a while to realize that he was still captive inside a big cage. For a while he kept on trying to find a way out, then he realized that the men were gone, and he came to a stand, looking at the details of his surroundings.

Everywhere he looked there were animals, some strange and some familiar; wolves, coyotes, wolverines, bears, even deer, which he looked at with none of his customary interest. They were all strangely mixed up showing no recognition of each other's presence.

Some loafed in the sun, other slept, still others paced back and forth endlessly, whiling away their boredom in the confines of their cages. A big fat grizzly sat on his broad rump grasping his upturned hind feet with the long claws of his front ones, rocking back and forth ceaselessly.

Kleo snarled, and reared against the restraining wall of his cage, suddenly leaping straight up in attempt to clear it, but he bumped his head hard on the heavy wire mesh top to fall back in an off-balance, ignominious scramble. Gathering himself up he made another circle of the cage, for the first time becoming aware of a trough full of clear water, which he ignored for a couple of more circles. On the next circuit his thirst got the better of him, and he stopped to lap up some of the cooling liquid — his first concession to being captive.

A heavy box with an open end, containing a layer of loose straw, was sitting in one corner of the cage, but he paid it no heed as he continued to prowl; nervous, restless and unable to comprehend the import of this great change.

All that night and the next day, he was continually in motion, his ears assailed by strange noises and his nose full of unusual smells. In the morning, the man who looked after the animals came and went quietly as he fed them. Finally he came close to the side of Kleo's cage trailing a hose, and the cougar faced him with an ugly snarl, exposing his teeth. The man did not back up, but only turned the hose on, filling the trough to the rim.

As he did so he admired the big cat, for this position was

more than just a job to him; he loved animals, they fascinated him — especially this wild cougar with his blazing eyes and powerful muscles rippling with every move.

Sometimes he had trouble keeping quiet about how the animals in his care were used in the motion picture productions, for this company specialized in so-called nature pictures that were in many ways anything but natural. Too often, in order to film some dramatic sequences, the animals were forcibly subjected to situations that they would never encounter in the wilds. Sometimes, as a result, they were badly injured or even killed.

Kleo's predecessor had been fatally injured when he was forced to jump off a cliff into a river. The desperate leap was short, ending up on rocks, and he was so badly hurt that it was necessary to destroy him. In the making of another picture at a desert location far to the south, the script called for a boar javelina to chase a bobcat up a giant cactus, something a bobcat would never tackle in the wild. A compound was built around a tall cactus, and in it were put a javelina and a bobcat. They could not avoid each other, and the cranky boar attacked the cat, finally killing it before it came anywhere near climbing the cactus. Before the required sequence was on film, the javelina had killed four bobcats. In the far north a polar bear cub was so badly injured that it died when it was pushed down a steep ice-covered slope so that its gyrations could be shot in slow motion.

Another time, during the filming of a squirrel picture, the keeper had been so filled with disgust when the teeth of two pine martens had been removed to prolong a killing scene, that he almost drew his pay and quit. The same operation had been conducted on the wolverine that he now fed hamburger every day, because it couldn't chew meat in chunks.

Of course, the people who saw the finished films never knew of the misery and cruelty suffered by the animals in them. They came in droves to applaud scenes that were beautifully filmed against spectacular backgrounds.

As he watched the big red-gold cougar turn away to pace along the far side of the cage, the keeper wondered what was in store for him.

For three days Kleo refused to eat the meat that was placed in the cage fresh every day. Never had he eaten anything he had not killed, but finally his hunger won out, and the keeper was happy when he saw that the proffered meat had been taken.

This acceptance of feed marked the beginning of a much improved relationship between the man and the big cat. Although always wary, Kleo began to accept the man to the point of even looking for his arrival. He also began to endure captivity without the endless prowling, sometimes taking shelter in the big nest box and sometimes lying on top of it half asleep, gazing off into the distance as though recalling the old, wild free days on the slopes of the mountains.

So it went for several weeks. Kleo's paw was completely healed and his coat was beginning to shine again.

Meanwhile an elaborate compound had been built on a ridge top among some spectacular rock formations which stuck up out of picturesque wind-twisted timber against the high jagged peaks of the background. It was to be the stage for an epic sequence.

One day the director summoned the keeper to give him some instructions involving the cougar. Kleo was to be placed in the compound. "When we get enough footage of the cougar moving around among the rocks and trees," the director told the keeper, "we'll put in a deer and wind it up with a killing sequence. It's a very important shot in this film and I hope that new cat will co-operate without holding things up. The producer's crying about expenses, so don't feed the cat for a couple of days. I want him hungry.''

Grim-faced, the keeper asked, "What deer are you planning to use?"

"That big mule deer doe. We've already got some shots of her, and she might be big enough to last longer and make the scene interesting. Prolonged action is what we need in this kind of scene," came the reply.

"But she's a pet! Everybody knows her around here and she'll eat out of anybody's hand," the keeper exploded. "Anyway, she'll last about two seconds if the cougar jumps her. She'll likely think he wants to play!"

"Maybe we can clip the cat's claws and make the scene last longer," the director suggested. "I don't give a damn about the deer. We pay to keep these animals so we can use 'em."

"If we trim that cougar's claws, sure as hell he'll sulk," the keeper stated angrily. "Don't forget, he was wild until we got him a month ago. Anyway, I'm sick and fed up to the neck with this trimming claws and pulling teeth business. One of these days the S.P.C.A. is going to drop on this outfit like a ton of rock, and I'm not so sure I won't cheer when it happens!"

For a long, tense moment, the two men glared at each other on the brink of an angry blow-up, but then the director sagged back in his chair.

"Don't forget," he said wearily, "that I don't write the script. And I just follow orders like everyone else around here. You have it your way about trimming the claws." Then he added, "But the rest of it goes. Shooting time is 10:00 A.M. two days from now if the weather is good. You just have the animals on location in time, and you can go somewhere where you don't have to watch."

The keeper left, feeling defeated and low in his mind, to feed the animals. That morning Kleo missed his fresh meat, and the keeper imagined he could see accusation in the cougar's green-gold eyes, as they watched him fill the water trough.

When he came to feed the mule deer doe, he scratched her ears and murmured, "For two cents I'd turn you loose. But you poor old scrounger, you wouldn't leave if I did." His face was grim as he went on with his work.

That night he couldn't sleep; he lay listening to his alarm clock ticking away the seconds. Somehow it sounded louder than usual. He was angry and sad at the same time, berating himself for getting too involved with the animals in his care. For about the hundredth time, he considered quitting, but rejected the idea. The job paid well, he needed the money and besides, someone else would take his place and they might not treat the animals right. Then he snorted at that idea, hating himself and his helplessness.

Finally, sometime after midnight, he got up, slipped his feet into a pair of moccasins and went outside. Back of the trailer camp, the peaks were standing black against a clear sky full of stars. It was windless, very quiet and pleasantly cool as he stood still letting the serenity soak into him if it would, while slowly puffing a cigarette.

Suddenly he threw the smoke down, stepped on it like he was killing some kind of objectionable bug and moved off toward the animal cages. Going into the cooling room where the meat was stored, he selected a choice chunk, which he carried to the cougar's cage, and opening the door, he threw it inside. He wasn't at all sure why feeding the cougar made him feel better, but it did. When he went back to his bed, he slept soundly for the rest of the night.

On time to the dot two mornings later, he drove the company four-wheel drive pick-up up to the shooting location with the cougar and the deer in separate trap boxes in the back. Backing into the compound, he released Kleo, watching him streak away to disappear among the trees and rocks. Then he drove out the gate, and carefully shut it before parking the truck out of sight and taking a position back of a tree to watch.

Kleo's first rush took him right across the compound and ended abruptly up against the fence. This fence was not only high, but was positioned to put any animal inclined to try to jump it at a disadvantage. To further discourage escape, three heavy barbed wire strands were strung in steel brackets projecting inward off the top of every post, forming an overhang. Kleo's exposure to wire had conditioned him to the futility of testing it, but even so he made a complete circle of the compound at the foot of the fence, before a man suddenly appeared to drive him away from it.

The enclosure was big and surrounded a heavily folded area of boulders, weather-worn turrets of rock and old, gnarled firs. Through this place, perhaps a hundred yards across, Kleo prowled back and forth, in and out, examining every detail of it, while six cameramen in hidden vantage points played their lenses on him as he moved.

The light was superb, and though unaware he was doing so, Kleo co-operated magnificently by posing here and there against the sky and mountains while the cameras rolled. The director hugged himself with delight, for what was being caught on film this day was rare and very valuable footage of an animal that normally chooses to move about only in the dark of the night.

Finally he lifted a bullhorn to his lips and called "Cut!" This was the signal to take the deer into the compound as the cameramen reloaded their cameras, making ready for the epic grand finale.

The days of preparation and high expense were about to be justified, the director fervently hoped. The animals were in place and the real action about to start. The cougar was still restlessly prowling, but the doe was singularly unimpressed when she caught sight of him against the sky on top of a rock rib.

She was lonely, and went poking slowly around here and there looking for company. Finally she located one of the cameramen, and happily started to climb up to him hoping for a handout, but he shied a rock off her ribs, driving her away, and likely making her wonder what had gone wrong with her world.

The tension built up among the camera crew as the two animals moved about out of sight of each other. Finally they chose converging paths that would bring the doe into the top of a short, steep draw and the cougar cutting across the mouth of it from the side. When they saw each other both animals froze, their eyes locked, at a distance of about ten yards. Then the hair rose on the deer's back and neck till she looked almost grotesque; her ears dropped, swinging loose on their sockets; she let out a sharp whistling snort, and went completely berserk. In two high long jumps she was over the surprised cougar, and came down with her feet bunched in the middle of his back, knocking him flat.

Two cameramen with the view in their finders couldn't believe what they were seeing, as the cougar rolled away to the side under the onslaught, but they kept shooting it anyway. Before Kleo could get his balance, the doe came down on him again, driving her weight like a pile-driver, her sharp punishing feet making him squall. If Kleo had been cornered he might have fought back, but as it was all he had in mind was getting away, so he came up running with the doe pounding along at his heels. Up and around and over the rocks they went, stirring up puffs of dust as they skidded in the turns. As he watched this astonishing melee, the keeper found himself silently cheering the big doe.

Kleo was hard pressed and desperate. When he came to a steep slope running down to the fence, he put on an inspired burst of speed and quit the rocks in a tremendous soaring leap — the highest and longest he had ever made in his life. His front feet caught the top, and there he clung, oblivious

167

to the sharp barbs as he reached for a purchase with his hind feet. One of them found a toe-hold and the next instant he was over the top and down the other side hightailing for open country at a wild run.

Behind him, the doe stood watching him go. Nobody knew it, but she had a history of such brawls. Picked up as a half-starved fawn, she had been raised on a ranch with a couple of dogs which, as she grew up, she treated as part of her life. But she absolutely refused to tolerate any other canines, and when a strange one showed, she instantly flew into a red-eyed rage. With typical deer tactics, she would leap high and come down on the surprised victim so effectively that she won every battle without exception. Finally a visitor's poodle was severely hurt by one of her onslaughts, and that was when she changed hands. She had treated Kleo as just another strange dog trespassing on her territory, and did not share the general surprise at his retreat.

Her hair flattened out, and her ears came up as she stepped out sedately to find somebody for company — somebody who wouldn't shy rocks at her and would maybe provide a handout. Meanwhile, behind his tree, the keeper bent down with tears of suppressed laughter running down his face, and off to one side of him, the director chewed his cigar and savagely tramped his cap into the ground.

The Friendly Owl

Charlie found him on the ground under a big cottonwood. How he came to be there will never be known. He was too small to have walked over the edge of the nest located thirty feet above. A look through binoculars from the top of a high bank on the other side of the creek showed another chick still in residence. Putting him back in the nest was considered, but the idea of braving the razor sharp claws of a pair of belligerent parent great horned owls held small attraction. So Charlie brought the little owl home; a small incongruous looking ball of white fluff that fitted easily into the palm of a hand, with small promise of ever looking like one of its big parents.

Thus Charlie became the godfather of a young horned owl, a turn of events which led to some mighty unexpected developments that nobody could have anticipated.

From the very beginning, we all agreed that if we were going to be responsible for raising this child of the wilds, it would not be confined in any way once it had learned to fly. If it ever chose to leave us, it would be free to go.

Charlie, having recently read some Greek mythology,

named the little owl Achilles, which was taking something of a chance, for at that age even a biologist would have had a problem identifying its sex. There was a fifty-fifty chance that a lady owl might some day find herself wearing a name that didn't fit. However, that was of small consequence.

We all knew that owls eat meat, but our research into the subject of owl diet told us that just meat was not enough. To be healthy and happy, a great horned owl needs some fur and feathers mixed in, for these collect around small bones accumulated in what goes for an owl's stomach, and are regurgitated. This process of throwing up pellets is an owl's way of putting out the garbage, and strangely enough they do not do well without it. With owls some very rough roughage is the name of the game.

Parent owls feed their young a wide variety of things; about everything in the small game line — even fish and reptiles on occasion. I once found the tail of a sucker on the ground below a nest, a big one that a parent owl had obviously taken from the shallow water on the edge of a beaver pond. So, almost any animal is acceptable grist for young owls' digestive mills. For a start, Charlie set out a trapline for mice, which Achilles accepted with great enthusiasm.

For his size, his appetite was prodigious, and it grew with him. At first he was too small to tear up the mice into pieces to fit his gullet, so Charlie performed this chore for him. Achilles would eat till there wasn't room for another morsel, subside into a contented ball of white fluff until the process of digestion made room, then wake up to ask for more. The supply of mice barely kept ahead of the demand.

At the time, Charlie and his older brother, Dick, were going to high school in town twenty-five miles away, and were boarding week days at a school dormitory. He wanted to take his adopted owl with him, and look after it in the room he shared with several other boys. This posed obvious

problems. We agreed to it as long as he got the necessary permission from the matron superintending the place, but we left the arranging up to him. With typical schoolboy philosophy, he concluded that what she didn't know wouldn't hurt her, so he smuggled Achilles into the dormitory.

Naturally every boy in the place knew about the owl, and with uncompromising gallantry and allegiance to broken rules, they kept the secret. Achilles became a sort of instant mascot, spending five days a week in a dormitory subsidiary to the halls of learning, and his weekends at the ranch.

Charlie's responsibilities reached a bit farther than anticipated, for the duties of keeping the room clean and neat were ordinarily taken in turn — two boys for each week — but it was unanimously agreed that in view of Charlie's owl, he would serve a permanent position on the clean-up team. This was a development he could hardly complain about, for Achilles' burgeoning appetite meant that he contributed a horrendous amount of reasons for cleaning — an aspect of nature paramount over all attempts to housebreak him.

The only refinement of toilet he ever practiced was to turn around when an urge of nature assaulted him while he was perched with his tail close to a wall. We were never quite sure if this was a habit learned or just instinctive. Maybe all owls practice this questionable amenity, but as he grew larger, and developed an unbelievable range and velocity to his ejections, we were of mixed thoughts on whether it was anything to brag about. When he suddenly turned around and lifted his tail, anyone standing within ten feet had better take cover!

With everybody contributing to the food supply, Achilles never went hungry, and he rapidly grew out of the shoe box that was his original nest, and was placed in a larger one. During classroom hours, he lived in a clothes closet, where his occasional chirps were sufficiently muffled not to carry to other parts of the house. The matron's inspection tours to check on the neatness of the room during the occupants' absence left her surprised at the unusual polish, but she did not find Achilles.

Achilles became more active as he grew. He rapidly learned to perch on things, and soon found the confines of a box annoying. When he was put out at something, he chirped loudly, a querulous complaining call very penetrating in its pitch, so Charlie worked hard to keep him happy. He got out of his box at every opportunity by hooking his beak over the edge and heaving himself up, with his claws scratching for a toe-hold. The hanger bar of the clothes closet made an ideal perch, so the clothing was pushed to one side to make room, and a makeshift partition made out of cardboard kept him from wandering on top of the apparel. A generous use of newspapers to accommodate the flotsam and jetsam that goes with a young owl helped in the housekeeping chores.

As the weeks passed the problems of keeping him enlarged with him. One morning after breakfast, Charlie placed him on his perch in the clothes closet as usual, and closed the door. But the catch did not quite engage, leaving a little crack of light showing, which undoubtedly intrigued Achilles. He leaned away over to inspect it, and overbalanced, to come tumbling down onto the floor. Chirping loudly, he waddled over to the crack, pushed his beak into it and the door swung open, allowing him to go out into the room. There he rambled about looking for company. The door leading to the hall and the top of the stairs was invitingly open, and Achilles proceeded to take a stroll.

Under the best of circumstances, an owl's feet are not designed for walking, and it moves in a mixture of steps and hops according to the footing and frame of mind, but when

Achilles came to the top of the stairs, he was faced with something of a dilemma. Undaunted he stepped over the edge of the top step and fell to the next. Getting up, he shook himself, proceeded to the next drop-off and launched himself again. His descent was rapid as well as unique, and he ultimately arrived at the bottom, somewhat ruffled but triumphant.

The good lady of the house was busy at her sink washing dishes, when her attention was drawn to strange noises coming from the stairway. She turned around just in time to see a very dishevelled young owl, with pin-feathers sticking out of his white fluff in every direction, come marching into her kitchen. She greeted him with a sharp exclamation of astonishment. He replied with a high-pitched chirp, and came to a stand swaying back and forth, his big eyes staring, and his round head swivelling from one side to the other on his skinny neck.

Some women would have gone into hysterics and yelled bloody murder for help, but not this one. She was the mother of several grown sons, and immediately guessed how it was that she had an owl in the house. Having grown up on a country farm, she lost no time in getting a large box and placing Achilles in it.

Actually, she was more than a little intrigued with the young owl, but rules being rules, when Charlie and his volunteer conspirators came charging in for lunch, she sternly confronted them. The following weekend saw Achilles come back to the ranch for good.

It was not long before his pin-feathers were transformed into feathers, and he looked less like an animated cartoon and more like a great horned owl. Just as soon as the big primary feathers of his wings grew out, he began to fly; short hops at first to be sure, with take-offs much better than the tail-over-teakettle wrecks that wiped out many of his landings; but it

174

was not long before he was doing much better, and he rapidly became a powerful and magnificently graceful flyer.

Although now a nearly full-grown bird with a certain imperious air when he chose — even a fierce look about him on occasion — Achilles was at heart a very gentle character with a tendency to be a real clown. While still afoot he had been installed on a perch on the veranda with plenty of old newspapers spread out under him to catch the inevitable droppings. Perhaps exposure to the written word triggered some kind of desire to amuse himself or whoever happened to be watching, but he learned to "read." He would jump down on a newspaper page and closely trace the letters across the columns with his beak in a way that was hilarious.

We were entertaining some guests one evening, and in due course they were introduced to Achilles. He came into our front room and perched on the back of a chair, regally looking at each of the strangers as though holding court.

Then Charlie threw a newspaper down on the floor in front of him, and he immediately flew down to go through his routine. In the middle of the front page there was a photo of a scantily clad beauty queen along with the account of her winning the contest. Achilles ran his beak along a line of print, and upon coming to the picture he reared back with a comical expression, and then bent forward as though unable to believe what he saw. Ruffling up his feathers till he looked twice his normal size, he swung his head back and forth, peering at the picture as though it assaulted his sense of propriety to the breaking point. The whole room dissolved in a gale of laughter.

Although completely independent in his movements, he was totalled dependent on us for feed. In the mornings he was always ravenous, and whoever showed up outside first was immediately greeted with a whole series of cheeps and chirps (his repertoire did not include hoots, which are the

175

call of a mature owl). So the first chore was to give him something to eat; a magpie or ground squirrel was best, for trying to fill him up on mice was next to impossible. He gulped them whole like so many raw oysters disappearing off a gourmet's plate, and we could not find enough to fill him. He tore up his own food now and would sometimes swallow astonishingly big pieces. We kept a supply of suitable things frozen in plastic bags in our freezer, which we thawed and gave to him as required.

One morning I gave him a magpie, whereupon he flew up to the peak of the gable on the end of our house, and proceeded to tear it up and devour it, feathers, bones and all. When he got to the wings, he did not separate them, but just ripped off the portion of the back to which they were attached, and proceeded to try to swallow it. He got it down to a point where a wing was sticking up on each side of his face like a grotesque moustache, and there it stuck. He humped his back, ruffled his feathers, braced his feet and gulped and gulped to no avail.

Finally he just stood still with his eyes almost closed, as though on the verge of death. Meanwhile I was watching from the lawn below, feeling helpless and wondering how long it would be before he came tumbling down from lack of oxygen. The question of how one would administer artificial respiration to an owl was crossing my mind, when he roused himself. Opening his eyes a bit, he reached up to grasp one of the protruding wings with a foot. He hauled the piece out and inspected it, then he put it down, pinning it against the roof, and began reducing it to more manageable pieces, pausing to give me a quizzical look when I burst into a roar of laughter.

He had a whole range of expressions — from extreme anger to sublime affection — according to his mood of the moment. Although he had associated with people exclusively, and undoubtedly related himself to us to some extent, as he grew older it became more and more apparent that he was all great horned owl and intended to remain so.

He and Seppi, our German shorthaired pointer, largely ignored each other, but he loved to tease our cat. Although the cat affected some tolerance, it was afraid of him. Achilles did nothing to reassure the cat, for one of his tricks was to fly at it from the rear as it crossed the lawn, planing in close on his incredibly silent wings. Becoming aware of the owl only when its widespread wings were directly overhead, the cat would let out an explosive hiss and high-tail for the nearest cover. This seemed to amuse Achilles, for he would land on the nearest thing sticking up from the ground, and squawk as though inviting the cat out for more play.

From the moment he took to the air, we were aware of his absolutely phenomenal vision. One afternoon I was reading in a deck chair on the veranda with Achilles perched at my elbow. For a while he amused himself by "reading" the pages as they were turned, but then he subsided to sit with eyes almost closed. Suddenly he came fully awake, tense in every fibre as he looked up into the sky. The very slow turning of his head indicated that he was watching something on the move, but I could see nothing. Picking up my binoculars, I trained them on the seemingly empty sky where he was looking. At first I still couldn't see a thing, but then the nine power lenses picked up a tiny moving dot — a golden eagle soaring away up at an altitude of thousands of feet.

Another day I was replacing a post in the yard fence while Achilles looked on from a convenient perch in a tree. When I got the new post set, and had fastened the wire to it with staples, he flew down to land on it, peering this way and that in a comical fashion as though passing inspection on my work. Abruptly he tensed, looking off into the sky past the top of our hill, and before I could more than turn my head in that direction, he flopped down onto the ground on

177

his back with every feather standing on end, his wings spread and his great talons extended upwards. Almost instantly, a powerful goshawk spun by, barely missed the top of the post within six feet of me, shot up a hundred feet to turn, looking down at Achilles, then flew away over the trees out of sight. The goshawk had been in a sizzling stoop, likely going at a speed of over a hundred miles per hour — a strike that would have killed the owl immediately if it had connected. It was an electrifying and unusual opportunity to observe the violent interaction between two formidable predators.

Crows reacted violently to the owl's presence, and it was not unusual for us to wake up early in the morning to the sounds of a riot going full swing, as a flock of them dived and swore at him where he sat perched in a tree. Beyond keeping an eye on them, he largely ignored them, but if one came too close, he would pop his beak angrily, loudly and rapidly. In the wilds it is evident that great horned owls prey on crows, probably at night, and they are implacable enemies. We never saw Achilles make any attempt to fight back when they harassed him, probably because they were on the wing most of the time. Horned owls do not take their prey on the wing as hawks and eagles occasionally do, but strike them from a tree or on the ground. In self protection from the ear-shattering bedlam, one of us usually went to the rescue, our presence driving the attackers away, whereupon Achilles would look down, shake himself as though happy with the return of quiet, and squawk querulously.

Heat bothered him, and in the middle of summer days, he would sit in a shady place with his wings spread a little to let the air under them, and his beak half open. On such days he was almost completely inactive. But toward sunset, when it began to cool, Achilles would come planing in from some bower in the tree tops to join us. He treated strangers with equal friendliness, but we always warned visitors of his presence. It is a bit unnerving to have a great horned owl appear unexpectedly, flying straight at you with his big yellow eyes gleaming, and land on the arm of your chair or on your shoulder. Even when visitors were alerted, Achilles' arrival never failed to give them a thrill, sometimes to our embarrassment.

One afternoon we were entertaining several VIPs — the president and top executive officers of a famous international conservation organization. After dinner, we all went out to sit on the big veranda to watch the sunset over the mountains spread out in front. I told them not to be surprised if a great horned owl flew in to join us, and not to jump away if he landed on a shoulder, for this would throw Achilles off balance, and if he used his talons to regain it the result might be painful.

I doubt that some of the group took me very seriously, but Achilles did not fail me; he suddenly showed up, and set his wings to glide in for a landing on the president's shoulder. The gentleman from New York flinched involuntarily as Achilles spread his wicked looking talons to land, throwing him a bit off balance. When Achilles reached out with a foot to steady himself, one of his razor sharp talons cut a neat, shallow gash about an inch long just over our visitor's collar on the side of his neck. For a moment we were all frozen, and then Achilles flew over onto the arm of my chair happily chirping and twitching my sleeve playfully.

The president was understandably a bit incredulous and startled at this turn of events, but he was a good sport about it as we patched him up with some disinfectant and a small bandage.

Following this incident, Achilles and our five-year-old daughter proceeded to entertain us with a game they regularly played. Wearing nothing more than a thin T-shirt and a pair of jeans, she ran down the slope below the front steps for a hundred feet or so, and hid in the tall grass, whereupon Achilles launched himself high on a long swing over the hillside to look for her. Suddenly he peeled off into a fierce strike, coming down with claws fully extended as though to kill. But his landing on her little rump as she lay flattened out in the grass was as light as thistledown. With eyes half closed, squeaking happily, he walked up her back to gently pull her pony-tail, and tweak her ears with his beak as she giggled at his tickling. He left her to fly back up to the arm of my chair, while she hid somewhere else. As soon as she was still, he repeated the performance, and as always, it was a bit hair-raising to see the fierceness of his strike, even though it always ended up in the gentlest possible contact. In spite of thin clothing and the numerous times they played this game, he never marked her tender skin with his fearsome claws, indicating an incredible degree of control on his part.

Our visitors were impressed in more ways than one. When they left, they were still talking about the experience. I heard later that the president made the scar a sort of conversation piece, showing it proudly to his friends.

As time went on we were aware that Achilles was widening his range well outside the perimeter of our yard, even though his appearances at feeding time were prompt. This put him in some danger, for if he chose to fly up to a complete stranger, his friendliness might easily be mistaken for an attack — with dire results. It also became apparent that he would go back to the wilds if he could learn to feed himself.

Surprise could be in his favour. One day, shortly after noon lunch, I stepped out to look down over a neighbour's field about half a mile down in the valley. Their new hired man was making a first cut around the edge of the hay crop with a power mower, the sound of the tractor humming along coming very clearly on the still air. Achilles was sitting on the back of a chair nearby with his eyes rivetted on the moving machine, obviously interested in it.

Something plugged the cutter bar, and the man stopped the tractor to clear the obstruction. At that point, Achilles took off in a long glide down over the treetops. Quickly picking up my binoculars, I watched as he arrived at the tractor, and landed on the back of the seat. As always, his flight was absolutely silent and the man was unaware of him until he straightened up to climb back onto the tractor and found himself eye to eye with a formidable looking owl that squawked at him. He jumped straight back about three feet and it was lucky for Achilles that he didn't have some kind of weapon to throw or swing. For a long moment the tableau was frozen, and then Achilles took off to come winging back.

A couple of hours later I talked to the hired man, who was Danish and spoke with a heavy accent. He was still excited about his adventure and had some difficulty finding words to describe his encounter with the owl. He was even more astonished when I told him about Achilles, and assured him that the big bird was very friendly, even if a bit sudden sometimes about introducing himself.

Achilles was very active at night. His favourite perch was on top of a power pole in our yard, where we could hear him squawk. It commanded a wide expanse of lawn and nearby open ground, and I wondered if he was catching mice.

One evening I decided to test him. Taking a light spin-fishing outfit, I coloured a white practice plug to a neutral grey, and tied it on the end of the line. Then, standing out of Achilles' sight, I made a long cast out across the lawn. After a couple of slight twitches that moved the plug a bit in the short grass, Achilles came planing down off the top of the power pole to land on it and examine it with an expression of utter disbelief. What kind of nonsense was this? he seemed to ask, and I broke into laughter. This became a game between us, and always I was amazed at the keenness of his eyes. Rarely was it possible to more than twitch the lure before he saw it, even at a distance of well over a hundred feet. It was a sure thing that no mouse could move on the same ground without drawing his attention, although we never saw him take one.

As the fall progressed and the evenings became cooler, Achilles became more loquacious atop his favourite perch, giving forth raucous squawks very carrying in pitch. Occasionally we would hear the deep-throated hoots of mature owls somewhere off in the distance. The sound of his relatives excited Achilles, and he would snap his head around with his eyes fixed in the direction of the hoots.

Late one night when it was very dark, we became aware of two other owls in the trees around the house, and the yard was full of hoots and squawks. As suddenly as it began the excited owl conversation subsided into silence, and in the morning Achilles did not show up for his feed. We wondered if we would ever see him again.

Forty-eight hours later I walked out into the yard at sunrise to be greeted by an obviously starving Achilles. He flew down to land on my shoulder with a squawk, followed by a whole series of animated squeaks and chirps. When I moved as though to go away from the house, he dropped down onto my boot and tugged at my pant leg with his beak. When I got him a chunk of raw meat, he wolfed it down in great gulps, and asked for more.

He stayed with us for several days, then disappeared again. This time he was gone for nearly a week, and when he suddenly showed up one evening, there were two owls with him, calling from the shelter of the trees. Had his parents come back to claim him? There was no way of knowing, but most certainly the presence of the other owls was no coincidence. We noticed some change in Achilles, for he had obviously found feed, and there was a marked aura of

182

independence about him that told us that he was returning to the wild. He accepted feed, but with a kind of diffidence, as though letting us know that he could now fare for himself.

When he left again, we thought he was gone forever.

Late one night, as I was driving home through a new fall of snow, my car slipped off the shoulder of the road into the ditch. I left it and continued on foot in the moonlight. Within three hundred yards of the house, where the road wound through a grove of cottonwoods, a big owl came suddenly winging down to land on my shoulder. Achilles greeted me as always with a whole string of happy cheeps and chirps, and rode on my shoulder to the house, where I gave him a piece of raw steak. He tore it up, and ate it with his usual gusto, demonstrating an unwavering appetite, and an ability to swallow chunks that looked big enough to choke him.

In the morning he was still there, and I presented him with a fresh magpie. When the moon came up full and round that evening, lighting up the snow-draped hills and mountains spread out before our ranch buildings in glittering splendour, Achilles was perched atop his favourite post. Charlie and I were out in the yard and we heard him give his raucous call. Faint and far off among the moonlit hills another great horned owl hooted in reply. Then Achilles took off, a black silhouette moving against a star-filled sky, fading rapidly in the distance.

We never saw him again. But even now, fifteen years later, when we hear a great horned owl call, we are reminded of a friend we once knew, a gentle spirit of the wild country whom we loved.